S. CUTHBERT'S CHURCH.

Frontispiece.

The Fellowship of the Veld.

THE FELLOWSHIP
OF THE VELD

SKETCHES OF NATIVE LIFE IN
SOUTH AFRICA

BY

GODFREY CALLAWAY, S.S.J.E.

WITH PREFACE BY THE BISHOP OF ZULULAND

WITH ILLUSTRATIONS

NEGRO UNIVERSITIES PRESS
NEW YORK

BR
1450
.C3
1969

Originally published in 1926
by the Macmillan Company

Reprinted 1969 by
Negro Universities Press
A DIVISION OF GREENWOOD PUBLISHING CORP.
NEW YORK

SBN 8371-1913-8

PRINTED IN UNITED STATES OF AMERICA

PREFACE

TO be asked to write a preface to Father Callaway's book is an honour which I cannot
decline. For his sincerity of purpose, his
long experience, and his powers of describing Native
life and character from a Christian point of view,
combine to produce a book that gives, to those who
wish to understand, vivid impressions both of what
is on the surface and what lies beneath. And the word
fellowship indicates the true Missionary spirit : not the
ability merely to maintain discipline, valuable as that is :
nor sentimental affection for the black people ; but such
a tender and wise attitude as the priest and pastor, and
others too, should have for those whom they know
and among whom their life is spent : not showing them
as anthropologically interesting or successful subjects
of evangelistic experiment, but as fellow-members
of the Christian family, sharers in the Sacrament of
Holy Fellowship, inheritors of the same Kingdom,
fellow-labourers in the same cause : different from us
in the God-given variety of the human race, with
methods of mind and reasoning in many ways unlike
those of the European, but shown as capable of and
exercising Christian, as well as natural, virtues, and
breathing freely in the atmosphere of Catholic faith
and practice.

From personal experience, I can testify to the

accuracy of these pictures of life, and the reality of the sense of fellowship. The Missionary who is really a Shepherd, and not merely an Umlungu (white man), is easily discerned by the Native, heathen as well as Christian ; he knows, sometimes fully, sometimes dimly, the dark places in the Native life, but recognises that, beneath the dust and dirt of superstition and ingrained custom, there is the coin with the Image of God, which the servant of Christ seeks diligently, finds, and places—cleansed by the Spirit and by careful teaching—in the Crown of our Lord, in the fellowship of His Body who is the Lover of men.

If this book has the very wide circulation and reception that I wish for it earnestly, it will be a beacon light to many a young Missionary, and give to readers in South Africa and in Europe alike illustrations of what Missions are doing, and the true aspect of their work.

WILMOT ZULULAND.

WHITSUN EVE, 1924.

AUTHOR'S PREFACE

BY request I have collected in this volume a number of little papers which have been written from time to time during the last fifteen years. Most of them have been published in the *Cowley Evangelist;* a few in *The East and the West* and the *Star in the East*; and to the Editors of these magazines I am grateful for permission to republish them in book form.

In writing these papers I had no intention of producing a book, and this will explain why there is sometimes a repetition of thought and even of language. There is, nevertheless, I venture to think, a central thought which runs through them and links them together. This it is which enables me to publish them under the title, *The Fellowship of the Veld*.

The Missionary who comes to South Africa is faced by the deep contrast between the primitive order and European civilisation. He cannot say that the one is all good and the other all bad. He is forced to weigh, to compare, and to contrast the two social orders. As he looks at the primitive society he may see much that is wild, capricious, and even savage ; but he also sees much that is excellent, much that tends to the content and happiness of the people. He sees fellowship. From this primitive society he turns with new freedom to criticise the civilisation in which he himself has been nurtured.

v

Montaigne found so many virtues in the social life of the primitive inhabitants of Brazil that he actually sought to excuse their cannibalism. He found greater fault in the civilised world, where practically nine-tenths of the people were "serfs." "Is it not worse," he asks, "to eat one's fellow-man alive than to eat him dead?" Perhaps he smiled as he asked the question, but behind the smile there was a challenge.

We do not want to follow Montaigne to such extremes, but we do want eyes to see all that is of permanent value in the primitive order. We want to be careful not to sweep away too freely the customs of the past, not to allow blind imitation of things European.

We want to ask how far Christianity may be presented as the fulfilment of the primitive order. What is there in that primitive order which will dispose the people to accept Christianity? Possibly such questions may find some answer in the following pages.

My warm thanks are due to the Bishop of Zululand for his kindness in commending this little volume ; to the Rev. R. A. Scott for most kind help in revision ; to Miss F. Oakeshott for the generous work of typing the whole ; and to various friends for photographs.

To readers who do not see the *Cowley Evangelist* or the *Star in the East*, I may mention that St. Cuthbert's Mission of the Diocese of St. John's, Kaffraria, where I have found all my experience, is in the heart of the Transkei—a large Native Reserve between Natal and Cape Colony proper. In that Reserve live a million Xosa-speaking Natives of various tribes.

GODFREY CALLAWAY, S.S.J.E.

CONTENTS

CONTENTS

PART III

THE NEW FELLOWSHIP

LIST OF ILLUSTRATIONS

ix

THE FELLOWSHIP OF THE VELD

FELLOWSHIP IN THE SANCTUARY—A MEDITATION

" What if earth
Be but the shadow of Heaven and things therein
Each to other like, more than on earth is thought ? "

" Behold, He cometh leaping upon the mountains."
CANT. II. 8.

THE Sanctuary is just one great encircling sweep of the Drakensburg Mountains, and the width of the apse, from Xalanga peak to those lofty piers of rock on the further side of Elliot, cannot be far short of forty miles.

Rain is rare in winter, but one day recently it fell in torrents, and we knew that the heights of the Sanctuary would be robed in Festal white. That was on the Feast of Corpus Christi.

One day, shortly after this, I went out early in the morning. The sky was absolutely clear and cloudless. The crescent of the waning moon hung, still glittering, in a grey-blue sky. The great walls of the Sanctuary rose up from the shade of the valley to support the vast vault of heaven, with ramparts domed with snow. " And it shall come to pass in the last days that the mountain of the Lord's house shall be established in the top of the mountains, and shall be exalted above the hills." Over the spacious floor of the Sanctuary was spread a carpet of purest white, laid by the frost of a winter night. Upon that carpet no foot had left its print.

Within the Sanctuary I saw neither Priest nor Altar. "Lord, who shall dwell in Thy tabernacle : or who shall rest upon Thy holy hill ? Even he that leadeth an uncorrupt life. . . ." Such a Sanctuary is for the uncorrupt—for the Saints alone. How can man, so conscious of his sin, dare to set foot on such a floor —to lift his eyes to such hills ?

" Enter into the rock, and hide thee in the dust, for fear of the Lord, and for the glory of His majesty.

" The lofty looks of man shall be humbled, and the haughtiness of man shall be bowed down, and the Lord alone exalted in that day.

" For the day of the Lord of Hosts shall be upon every one that is proud and lofty, and upon every one that is lifted up ; and he shall be brought low."

" There was neither speech nor language, but their voices," the voices of those silent, still, snow-robed mountains, forbade approach. They declared in the innermost depths of the heart the penalty of sin, the need of abasement.

" Give sentence with me, O God, and defend my cause against the ungodly people ; O deliver me from the deceitful and wicked man.

" For Thou art the God of my strength, why hast Thou put me from Thee : and why go I so heavily, while the enemy oppresseth me ?

" O send out Thy light and Thy truth that they may lead me : and bring me unto Thy holy hill, and to Thy dwelling."

It was not, on this occasion, the cry of the vested Priest bowing in the Sanctuary and saying his *con-*

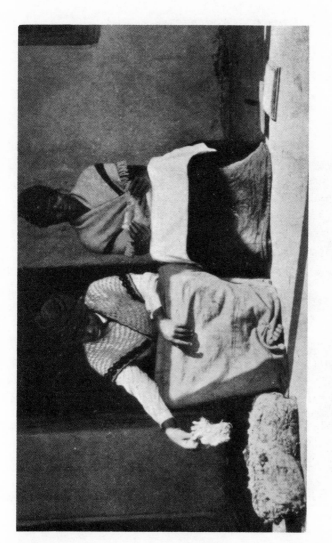

WOOL-CARDING AT ST. CUTHBERT'S WEAVING SCHOOL.

facing p. 2.

ROLL CALL. BOY'S BOARDING SCHOOL. ST. CUTHBERT'S.

facing p. 3.

fiteor before ascending the steps of the Altar. It was the cry of one listening to the ceaseless proclamation of the holiness of God. " And one cried unto another and said; Holy, holy, holy, is the Lord of Hosts." " Holy, holy, holy "—that is what the beautiful mountains declared. That is what the silence and stillness declared.

It was the cry of a soul conscious only of her sin, a soul waiting for the " Lamb of God that taketh away the sins of the world "—waiting for the Priest and the cleansing word of absolution.

There was, it seemed, no Altar, no Lamb of God that taketh away the sins of the world, no Priest, no absolution. It is true that there was no *visible* barrier to access, no " flaming sword which turned every way."

But there was no invitation to the weary and sin-laden soul, no " comfortable words " declaring the love of God who " gave His only-begotten Son that whosoever believeth in Him should not perish but have everlasting life."

There was no message of a " true saying, and worthy of all men to be received, that Christ Jesus came into the world to save sinners."

It was just the " *holy* hill "—unutterably holy.

* * * *

There was a slight change of colour in the sky towards the east. Into the dread purity of the sky shot a warm glow—as from Calvary. Gradually the glow spread up over the whole of the eastern canopy.

It was the herald of a coming Presence.

As I saw the glow I did not say, " Surely the Lord is in this place." I had said that long before. I said, " Surely the mercy of the Lord is in this place and I knew it not. Surely the merciful Priest who can be ' touched with the feeling of our infirmities ' is here. Surely the Hand outstretched to save and to absolve is here. Surely the Altar of Sacrifice is here—and I knew it not ! "

" But unto you that fear My name shall the Sun of righteousness arise with healing in His wings."

Slowly the Host appeared within the Sanctuary, elevated for adoration. Light, brilliant and dazzling, leapt into the shade of the Sanctuary. The carpet shone, and every single fibre of it shone, like diamonds in a blaze of light.

Slowly the mist-cloud of the valley rose like a cloud of incense, and was caught and transfigured by the rays of light—or rather it gave form and substance to the light.

> " Lo, in the sanctuaried east
> Day, a dedicated Priest
> In all his robes pontifical exprest,
> Lifteth slowly, lifteth sweetly,
> From out its orient tabernacle drawn,
> Yon orbed Sacrament confest
> Which sprinkles benediction through the dawn."

" The voice of my Beloved ! behold He cometh leaping upon the mountains, skipping upon the hills.

" My Beloved is like a roe or a young hart : behold He standeth behind our wall, He looketh forth at the windows, showing Himself through the lattice.

" My Beloved spake, and said unto me, Rise up, my love, my fair one, and come away.

" For, lo, the winter is past, the rain is over and gone ; the flowers appear on the earth ; the time of the singing of birds has come. . . ."

*   *   *   *

Θεοῦ τὸ δῶρον—" Of God the gift." The wealth is unlimited. No outlay can reduce it. It is for all, and no one is outside it. We alone can bar from ourselves the flow of that stream of mercy. There are times when we feel that we cannot make our approach to the Sanctuary. The floor is pure white, and soiled by the faintest tread of sinful man. There are times when we feel that we cannot take home to our hearts the assurance of God's forgiveness—the comfort and joy and gladness of it until . . . until we are more completely dead to sin, until all pride has been absolutely killed, until self is wholly mortified.

Θεοῦ τὸ δῶρον. It is just by the power of the forgiveness of God that we shall alone be able to die to sin and self. It is as we joyfully welcome the forgiveness and mercy and love of God that we find ourselves enabled to seek the lowest place, and, therefore, able to join with the mountains of the Sanctuary and with the silence of early dawn, with angels and archangels and all the host and company of Heaven in saying, "Holy, Holy, Holy, Lord God of Hosts. Heaven and earth are full of Thy glory. Glory be to Thee, O Lord most high."

PART I

FELLOWSHIP WITH NATURE

CHAPTER I

BROTHER SUN AND SISTER WATER

" The land . . . is a land of hills and valleys and drinketh water of the rain of heaven :
" A land which the Lord thy God careth for."

DEUT. XI. 11, 12.

" Praised be Thou, O Lord, of all Thy creatures and above all of Brother Sun, my Lord, that doth illumine us with the dawning of the day. For fair is he and bright, and the brightness of his Glory doth dignify Thee, O Thou most Highest.
" Praised be Thou, O my Lord, of Sister Water, for manifold is her use, and humble is she and precious and chaste."

ST. FRANCIS OF ASSISI.

Ilanga libalele

(The Sun scorches—there is a drought)

WE, too, out here on the veld have our *imbongi* (poets), who improvise songs of praise, but so far as I am aware the *izibongo* (poems) are limited to the praise of chiefs and famous men. Yet it is difficult to think that an African poet would have no praise for Brother Sun, to whom he owes so much and in whose warmth he wraps himself as in a

7

garment for most of the days of the year. The African is essentially a child of the sun. Look at him as he begins the serious schooling of life as a pupil or fag of his elder brothers in herding his father's sheep and goats. What a great day that is when, proudly conscious of his inalienable privilege as a man child, he sallies forth to a life full of wild adventure! There are for him no intricacies of laced boots and overcoats, no maternal injunctions to keep his feet dry and to take care not to soil his nice clean clothes. There he is clothed in a beautiful, smooth, brown skin, unashamed. He may roll in the muddiest of muddy pools and no one will say him nay. Is there not above him a glorious bright sun which serves for towel to dry him, fire to warm him, clothing to wrap round him?

And when he passes out of the golden days of childhood into the serious and responsible days of manhood, he is still a child who basks in the sun, and bathes in the sun, and dries in the sun, and thrives in the sun. That must indeed be a strange City which has "no need of the sun to shine upon it"! No Native would feel drawn towards such a city, until he went on to learn that the "countenance" of the Chief of that City is "as the sun which shineth in his strength." Surely the *imbongi* is at fault if he has no word of praise for Brother Sun.

At times, however, Brother Sun would come in for some very hard words from the *imbongi*. When Brother Sun is not on speaking terms with Sister Water and drives her from his presence, then indeed he becomes an enemy.

Out here when we salute one another we invariably ask after one another's health. It would be lacking in a proper respect towards your neighbour to manifest no anxiety as to his bodily welfare. The first question

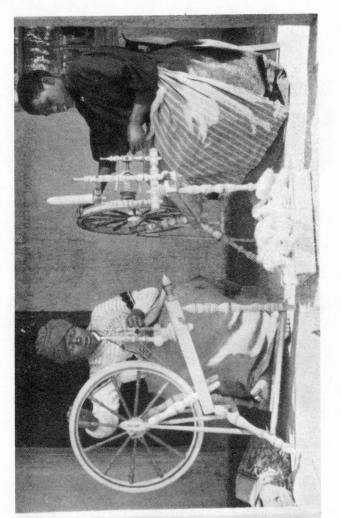

SPINNING AT ST. CUTHBERT'S WEAVING SCHOOL.

facing p. 8.

THE WATER FALLS IN SEPARATE GRACEFUL STREAMS.

facing p. 9.

always is, " Usapila na ? " ("Are you well ? "). One day the answer came to me : " Ndisapila : andipili noko ; lilanga eli," which, being literally translated, means, "I am well ; but I am not well ; it is this sun."

What would the stranger make of this answer ? I can imagine he might edge away from the speaker with some degree of nervous apprehension. He would probably jump to the not unreasonable conclusion that the man was suffering from sunstroke, and was affected in his head.

As a matter of fact, the man is only stating in a very characteristic way that, although he as an individual. is well, yet he is not well, because he is sharing in the one dominating and dire affliction of the community, and that affliction is the sun ! The sun, which comes forth day by day as a royal "bridegroom out of his chamber, and rejoices as a giant to run his course," has become the enemy. Brother Sun has quarrelled with Sister Water, and has banished her from his presence. Day after day those fierce rays beat down with pitiless power upon the parched ground until the grass, which has bravely struggled to maintain its life, appears to give up the struggle and to die down to its roots. It is then that the earth seems to take up her lamentation and utter her reproach against man, "Have I not been a faithful servant ministering to thy wants ? When have I failed thee ? Why now dost thou fail me ? Why hast thou not pleaded my cause and voiced my agony ? " The herds wander further and further afield in search of pasture, until the weakest lie down to die. From them too, from out of patient, pleading, suffering eyes, comes reproach against man. On all sides we seem to hear a sad-toned litany of supplication : " The whole creation groaneth and travaileth in pain." It is true that it travaileth in hope, but "hope deferred maketh the heart sick." Day follows day ; month follows month. Clouds may gather in the sky, but only mock with promises not fulfilled. "All the merry-hearted do sigh. . . . All joy is darkened, the mirth of the land is gone." Is it surprising that the one thing that seems to matter is rain—Sister Water ? Everything hinges upon that. All else is secondary. Religion itself is being weighed in the balance. If religion counts at all it must count here. It is no use talking about other matters. Elijah was quite right. There is only one test between Jehovah and Baal, between the inherited beliefs of the past and the new teaching in the Missions.

The *Abatwa* (Bushmen) are more or less discredited because they failed in this one crucial test. Christiani .y —so speaks the man of the veld—must not avoid the test. It must be proved true or false. You may talk about the lessons of suffering, the purpose of trial, the beneficial effect of affliction, but in his heart of hearts the Native thinks you are refusing the challenge. He may be too polite to give expression to his thoughts, but he remembers that when the sky was "settled fair " and the Bushmen wanted to gain time, they used to try by every artifice to defer the test.

"Bawo, siyabulawa lilanga " (" Father, we are being killed by the sun "). The words are not spoken with impatience and anger. On the contrary, I am amazed at the self-restraint of the speaker. He sees his cattle dying and his children suffering from lack of food, yet speaks in a self-controlled and patient way. Such restraint is part of the " good form " of Native life. It is *ngokusesikweni*, according to code and good and proper custom. It belongs to the " manliness " taught in the circumcision school.

Yet as I listen I feel that there is at least a latent

reproach. This is what they seem to say, " Father, you are our shepherd, do you not see the distress of your flock ? It would be wanting in respect on my part to think that you are incapable of help. Do I not believe that your prayer has power with God and prevails ? Why, then, is it that your flock is in such distress ? I will not go on to suggest a reason, but I do ask you to think deeply yourself."

The words seemed to reach like a swift-winged arrow into the inner citadel of conscience. Is not the shepherd responsible ? Is there no mysterious correspondence between the drought without and the drought within the soul of the shepherd ? When the Psalmist of old tried to describe the misery of a burdened conscience, did he not instinctively turn to the drought-stricken land ? " For Thy hand is heavy upon me day and night ; and my moisture is like the drought in summer."

> " My heart is withered like a ground,
> Which Thou dost curse,"

cried George Herbert. At least the shepherd of the flock must see in the grievous drought a new call to repentance, a new invitation to open the doors of the soul to the streams of the living water.

True it is that the drought is also intended to make us look in other directions as well as to our own inner selves. Mother Earth may yield to coaxing even in times of drought, and the generous flowing streams which abound on the veld are still waiting the skill and labour of cunning hands, in order that they may give of their wealth to the sun-parched land. But when man has done his part to the utmost he is still but using the gifts of God, and the deep springs still look up to Him. " All my fountains are in Thee."

Amafu atambile

(Rain is plentiful)

Is it peace or war? These heralds who sally
forth in advance of the main body, do they come to
open battle, or are they the envoys of a gracious
succour? Look at them as they soar over the rugged
crest of the Kwanca Mountain. Magnificent they are
indeed, but heavy, and dark and ominous.

The answer is not long in coming. The challenge
rings out quick, and sharp, and menacing. In what
seems to be but the space of a moment the whole sky
is hidden, and with a heavy roar behind it, down comes
Sister Water. The long-looked-for rain comes, but
it comes as if with fierce and passionate anger. It
comes like the bombardment of an enemy rather
than the gracious gift of a friend. It comes as if after
some desperate struggle it were hurled by the hand
of some vindictive power. It was just as if some
ill-disposed tyrant had been possessed of God's gracious
gift of rain. Callous in the presence of suffering,
unmoved by entreaty, he " keepeth his palace and his
goods are in peace." But a champion stronger than
he had arisen to defend the fatherless and widow, to
relieve the oppressed and to overthrow the tyranny
of the oppressor. Fierce had been the conflict. Des-
perately wounded, the tyrant had been forced to yield
up his ill-gotten spoils. Even while he did so he
rained down fierce and fearful maledictions, livid
flashes of white fury. " The earth trembled and
quaked : the very foundations of the hills shook and
were removed because He was wroth. There went a
smoke out of His Presence and a consuming fire out
of His mouth, so that coals were kindled at it."

As suddenly as the bombardment had begun so

suddenly for the moment did it cease. On the third day all signs of the conflict had disappeared and the full fruits of the victory were made manifest. Smooth and soft-curved clouds settled down on the neighbouring hills, gradually hiding them from sight. Gently now Sister Water made her approach as if with apologies for the terrible turmoil of the past. She came like the benediction of a merciful Father. She came to cleanse, to soothe, to comfort, to strengthen.

Almost with a hush of awe and reverence men listen, after a long drought, to the music of the rain falling gently on the dry foliage and hot, parched earth. They listen to the splashing of the drops from the roof and to the pleasant sound of the running streams. With a deep sigh of satisfaction they abandon themselves to the joy of relief. No questions are asked, no reproaches uttered. Sister Water has come. We do not say, " Why hast thou tarried so long ? Why hast thou thus dealt with us ? " We open wide the door of welcome.

Amafu atambile (the clouds are soft, rain is plentiful), says the Native, and he settles himself with new-born comfort upon his mat ; he finds new fragrance in his pipe, and new solace in the conversation of his friends.

As a fortright ago, I sit looking at the same mountains, the same rolling waves of veld, the same ridges dotted with the kraals of the people. A fortnight ago I seemed to see a face withered and worn and hard, a face from which all light and peace had fled. It was as the face of one sin-bound, unable to find rest or relief. " Thy Hand was heavy upon me day and night." Everything told the same story of a soul troubled and ill at ease, worn with the bitter sense of estrangement. I looked at the sun-baked mountains, the long ridges of dry veld, the flocks gaunt and famine-pressed. I read everywhere bitterness and fierce resentment. " The whole creation groaneth and travaileth in pain." To-day, it is the face of a friend who smiles, who laughs, who sings, who loves. A great reconcilation has taken place. I see a " new creation." The " spirit of heaviness " has fled away and has been exchanged for the " garment of praise." The mountains and hills " break out into singing " and all the trees of the forest " clap their hands." Brother Sun himself shares in the great reconciliation. The warm moist earth flashes a glad response to his rays.

It is Sister Water through whom the transformation has come. " Praised be Thou, O my Lord, of Sister Water, for manifold is her use, and humble is she and precious and chaste."

CHAPTER II

WEALTH (*INDYEBO*)

"Ploughlands, scarred for certain grain."

"GRANDMOTHER," said I to an old woman, "how do the crops look in your land?"
"Parts of them are not so bad, Father, but the sun of last month scorched the earlier crops and the grub has got into the later crop."

Unless you knew the fashion of speech you would think, both from manner and words, that the prospect was fairly bad, and you would begin to commiserate.

"Is that your land, Grandmother, that I pass on my way to B——'s kraal?"

"Yes, Father, that is one of them."

"Now look me in the face, Grandmother, and tell me the truth. Is there not *indyebo* (wealth—an exceptionally good crop) in your land?"

The old face suddenly seemed to lose its wrinkles and to be wreathed in smiles. "Father, we may think so in our hearts, but we don't like to say so."

That is just it—"we don't like to say so."

For years and years the crops have been a failure with, at the most, a very partial yield. Every penny earned by the young men at Johannesburg has been spent upon grain for the homes. Starvation has knocked so loudly at the door that at last they have to part with cattle. "I shut my eyes and parted with

a cow," as they say. And sometimes it was the only
cow and nothing short of the extremity of need would
have brought them to sell it.

This year (1923) there is a great and wonderful
promise. This morning I have ridden for miles along
a valley which laughs and sings with *indyebo* (wealth).
In our part of South Africa there are few marks of
private ownership of land. There is a happy sense of
κοινωνία (commonwealth). There are no fences or
walls or hedges. As I rode along this morning with a
gay heart—in spite of a burning sun—my path was,
in places, walled in on either side to the height of some
seven or eight feet, by the vigorous *ikaba* (plants at the
stage when the fruit is about to appear) of mealies and
kafir corn. I could well understand what it all meant to
the people who lived in those kraals on the sides of the
hills. It was almost too good to be true. The old
grandmother expressed the mind of all when she said,
" Father, we dare not speak of it." " There's many a
slip 'twixt the cup and the lip." A sudden hailstorm,
and down all that wealth would go as if reaped by a
ruthless sickle. And it is not only the people who
live in the kraals on the slopes of the hills who are
anxiously—most anxiously—watching that splendid
promise. The birds, too, have summed it all up.
They know exactly how long they must be satisfied
with scanty and less satisfying fare. They are looking
forward eagerly to the day when from out of those
lofty sheaves will emerge the head of tender grain of
kafir corn, which will fill out and ripen into red, meet
for the pouches of little birds. Oh yes, they know
that selfish man regards them as trespassers who have
no right to that kafir corn. They know that he
will build his little *amapempe* (temporary huts of grass
on a wattle frame), to which the young people will be
sent to watch against their depredations, but the birds

have long ago condemned these rigid, old-fashioned notions of private property and have proclaimed themselves communists. Nor will they be baulked of their rights by the cries of young folk. They know quite well that where *umlisela* (bands of lads) and the *umtinjana* (bands of lasses) get together there are golden chances for birds ! The mice, too, have joined the same " International " as the birds, and although they have not the same facility for reaching those tempting heads of grain, they pray for a beneficent wind-storm to lay low a few of those proud stalks and to bring the grain within the reach of hungry and deserving mice. At least one-half of the joy, both to birds and mice, is in the thought that they owe their feast to the hard labour and sweating toil of those dark-skinned capitalists who live in the kraals on the hills !

I wish I could describe it all. To my mind there is hardly anything I know to equal in beauty a field of maize at this particular stage. Branching out at regular intervals from the strong vigorous stalk are the graceful deep-green leaves which curl at the edge and taper off to a fine point. There are, perhaps, a dozen of these leaves to each plant, and each leaf must be about two feet long and four or five inches wide in the centre. With every slight breeze they swing and flutter, flashing radiant light. I almost seem to hear the whispering gentle song, " O all ye green things upon the earth, bless ye the Lord ! praise Him and magnify Him for ever."

> " Oh ! what was that gay scrap of song
> That made a music in the hills,
> More fleeting than the tender mist
> That all the sunlit valley fills ? "

Underneath, eagerly spreading out in every direction,

rioting in the warm earth and in the shelter of this
dense forest of stalks, are the trailing pumpkins already
bearing fruit.

My thoughts went back a few months to the time
when this sun-baked soil was being turned over by
the plough. That was the time when the red-crested
cuckoo (u-Pezukomkono, literally "he who is over
the arm") begins the cry which is regarded as the
signal for sowing mealies. And then, when the
young plants were a few inches above ground, began
the stern warfare with the weeds. Early in the
morning, before the sun peeped over the hills, all the
sound of limb, and even some who are not sound, would
shoulder the hoe and make for the lands. Standing
in long lines, with regular rhythmic motion, to the
accompaniment of a weird and monotonous chant,
their hoes would be plied throughout all the long hours
of the morning. Their labour this year promises to
be well rewarded. In many a land fruition has already
begun, and from the swelling side of the stalk the
young cob gradually detaches itself—except for the
primary attachment. At this stage it is just a closed
sheaf of numberless leafy wrappings, protecting the
young and delicate grain which begins to form on the
cob. *Umbona ubelekile.* The maize stalk is carrying
its cob, just as the mother carries her child on her
back.

Then from out of the end of the sheaf will come a
tassel of rare beauty, drooping and delicate, like the
fringe of the sea anemone.

In many parts of the country the heathen people
still await the word of the Chief before they begin to
pluck the ripening cobs. That word is spoken in
solemn assembly at the Feast of the First Fruits
(*ukushwama*). There is much to be said for a festival
of this sort, and the only pity is that it is so mixed

up with the craft of the witch doctor. It was intended, no doubt, to symbolise the figurative ownership of all land by the Chief, but it was of real practical value in restraining the people from a reckless use of the young and tender grain. . . .

My scattered thoughts were brought to an end. I had reached my destination and I was standing by the side of the solid stone walls, slowly mounting to completion, of a little church. Below me in the valley are the cultivated lands of the people, with their rich promise of *indyebo* (wealth). Some day, in the not very distant future, many of these people will be coming within these walls to eat the Food of way-farers—the living Bread. There it is that they will learn that the grain which they grow in their lands is symbolic of Jesus Christ.

It is always a matter of supreme interest to me that the word *umbona* (mealies) is unique in being personal —*he*, and not *it*. The younger generation is letting this personal use slip out, and I regret it. Mealies are the staple food of the country and will probably always continue to be so. It is the "bread" of the Native people, and I like to think that this personal use, *he* and *him*, links the word to the precious word of our Lord, "I am the living Bread." Remarkably do the Feasts of the Incarnation correspond to definite points in the growth of the mealie. Sown in the ground early in Advent, at Christmas it has entered by birth into the big world above ground. In Lent, or a little earlier, is the war with the hostile weeds which rapidly seek to occupy the soil before the mealies attain to strength. This war of the hoe corresponds to the war with temptation in the wilderness. At Easter it is the time of the firstfruits. "Christ is risen from the dead and become the firstfruits." At Pentecost is the harvest, when the ripe grain is brought home to be the bread of the people. My only regret is that the *umbona* (mealie), which is the corn of the country, cannot supply the bread which is to be broken upon the Altar of that little church to become the Body of Christ, the living Bread.* Here, in this Food, is the true *indyebo* (wealth) of the hungry soul, and here is no private ownership: the wealth is common wealth.

* Wheaten bread seems to have been required throughout the history of the Church.

PART II

THE PRIMITIVE FELLOWSHIP

CHAPTER III

HUMANITY (*UBUNTU*)

" He [the Native] is not in a position to estimate what
the technical conquests of nature mean as proofs of mental
and spiritual authority, but on one point he has an unerring
intuition, and that is on the question whether any particular
white man is a real moral personality or not."

" Neither children nor gods, but men in a world of men."

I

A NEW spirit of criticism is abroad throughout
the world. There was a day when the
Englishman would hardly have suspected
criticism on the part of the people of a backward
race. We ourselves turn the full glare of criticism
upon them, but we do not expect counter-criticism.
Generally speaking, the Englishman judged by an
external standard. He was conscious of a great gulf
which separated him and his civilisation and his
manners from the native people of a backward race.
When the immense width of this gulf has been nar-
rowed, when the Native has made at least many more

steps towards approximation to the European standard of culture, then comparison might possibly begin, but, in the meantime, the whole question might be dismissed.

Such an attitude carried with it a large measure of success, but the day for it is rapidly passing, chiefly because, all over the world, men are being judged by a new and less external standard. To the Native of these parts that standard would be known as *ubuntu*. When I look this word out in our excellent Xosa dictionary I find, " human nature or quality, humanity, kindness, manliness, manhood." Then comes a stroke of genius. It is just as if the compilers had been struggling to express a further and fuller shade of meaning and they go on to tell us what *ubuntu* is by describing the man who has lost it. Such a man is said to be " a common creature, worthless, contemptible ; *one who has thrown away the dignity of human nature.*"

Ubuntu, then, speaks to the Native of all that is most precious in the life of a people. Not of possessions external to the man, such as his cattle or his sheep, but of the best possession of all, the character of the people. Now I do not say that the white man, generally speaking, has lost *ubuntu*—the dignity of manhood. On the contrary, I should contradict such an assertion with my whole heart. In his home, in social life, in his own circle, the white man is kindly, generous, sympathetic. But the pity is that the Native does not, except on the rarest occasions, see the white man in his home nor in his social circle. Indeed, I will venture to say the whole mischief is that the Native does not see the white man at all. He does not see his *ubuntu*—the dignity of his manhood. What he does see, on the contrary, is the attitude of the white man towards himself, and in that attitude he reads the absence of respect for *ubuntu*.

Ubuntu implies a certain respect for the dignity of human nature itself, apart from the extraneous advantages of education, wealth, position, etc. A man is a person (*umntu*) and ought to be encouraged to realise the dignity of human nature. A man cannot despise another without harming himself, without doing despite to the human nature possessed in common with all other men. The complaint of the Native is just this, that the attitude of the white man towards himself denies his own *ubuntu*. The white man—so thinks the Native—does not respect *ubuntu*, human nature itself shared by all. He respects only certain outward advantages. If the white man reserved his contempt for what is essentially bad, it would be different. If he were to despise the thief as such, or the coward, or the drunkard, it would be intelligible. The Native himself does the same. But the white man's attitude implies contempt for the *ubuntu* of a whole people, and by that attitude he is condemning himself. In the eyes of the Native the white man is casting away the dignity of his own human nature.

Unhappily that attitude is instinctively adopted by the white man's child. He grows up into it naturally and inevitably. The child who is still too young to go to school is not too young to call the full-grown Native man " boy," and to shout his commands at him.

It is not work—not even the lowliest of all work—that degrades a man. It is to be forced into a position where a man is not free to be a man, and to exercise the reality of his manhood. Here it is that primitive ideas join hands with and find their sanction in Christianity.

To the thinking and more educated Native the puzzle of it all is, that the same white man who adopts the current attitude towards himself as a matter of course is a religious man. He goes to church : he observes Sunday : he welcomes the visits of a minister. But the puzzle grows larger the more the Native learns the content of that religion. Who is it who said, " I am amongst you as one that serveth " ? Who is it who exalted for all ages the title of Servant ? Who is it who said, " The Son of Man came not to be served but to serve " ? Who is it who said, " Blessed are the poor, the meek " ? Can these really be the words of the God whom the white men worship ? Can it be true that the white man treasures the teaching of the Apostle St. Paul ? Was it not St. Paul who said, " Have this mind in you, which was also in Christ Jesus : who, being in the form of God, counted it not a thing to be grasped to be on an equality with God, but emptied Himself, taking the form of a bond-servant " ? What a puzzle it all is !

It is not the least use to point out to the perplexed Native the splendid qualities of the white man, his reverence for truth, his sense of responsibility, his respect for a promise, his strict morality. All that may be unanswerably true, but the eyes of the Native are upon a quality which is dearer to him than any other. He wants to see respect for a fellow-man.

If Christianity does not produce this, he wants none of it—at least, he does not want the Christianity of the white man.

Ought we not really to be thankful that this is so ? Ought we not to be thankful for a criticism which is so wholesome ? It may pain and hurt us if we are willing to realise it, but this is a sign that God is calling us to judge ourselves, to bring our lives, our social conventions, our attitude towards our fellow-men under the only true Light—the Light which flows out from

THREE GENERATIONS.

facing p. 24.

BOYHOOD.

"THE WHOLE MANHOOD OF THE TRIBE."

facing p. 25.

the Life of Him whom we desire to honour, to follow and to love.

Surely there is only one way to meet and to overcome the extreme ideas which, beginning with the lawful assertion of the rights of the proletariat, end by tyrannising over all other rights. It is to learn to respect *ubuntu*, the dignity of human nature wherever it is found : " All that men ignored in me : this I was worth to God." Jesus said, " Whose is this image ? " . . . " Render therefore unto Cæsar the things that are Cæsar's, and unto God the things that are God's."

Ubuntu is really nothing else than the image of God stamped upon man, and by failing to respect that image we fail to respect God.

II

I have deliberately spoken of *ubuntu* from one point of view only, as representing the dignity of human nature inherent in every man. There is, however, an extended meaning of the word which in the dictionary is called " kindness." Personally I should be inclined to call it *neighbourliness*. To the Native the qualities which go to make up *ubuntu*, the qualities which make an *umntu* (person), are largely social. One would expect to find this in a people so corporate in outlook. The one essential law, the fulfilment and crown of all the other laws governing Native life, is that a man should be a neighbour. Just as the one law summing up all other laws for Christians is the " new commandment " that they should love one another, so to the Native the one supreme law is that he should be a neighbour.

Of all human beings the native of South Africa is surely one of the most sociable. Happiness for him " cannot be lonely : it is social, like humanity."

The Native is always on the look-out for *links* with others. Somehow or other he will succeed in establishing a relationship. If possible it will be a relationship of blood. It is a delight to him to be called, not by the name which belongs to him as an individual, but by the name which belongs to him as a member of a clan. It is in the possession of a clan name that he feels strong. He is no longer detached, and alone, and resting upon his own merits. He belongs to a clan, and therefore all that the clan possesses is his. He stands before the world arrayed perhaps in a red-ochred blanket, but also in the virtues and the dignity of the clan. To call him by his clan name creates a smile in his face. You are recognising his real dignity. By doing so you show, too, that you yourself are no stranger. You are adopting the native mind as your own.

The clan name will over and over again stand your friend in good stead. If he is in difficulty in a strange country his first thought is to find out some one who shares with him the clan name. In such a person he will find a brother. If there is no one who shares that kind of blood relationship, then he must look about for some other link, such as that of his wife's clan. His wife belongs to some other clan, and all the members of that clan were in a sense betrothed to him on the day of his betrothal to his wife. Of course, all the profits of the contract cannot be on one side. The helpfulness must be mutual, and, indeed, I have never found a Native to deny such obligation. The " poor relation " who is shunned and evaded and kept at arm's length in European society does not exist amongst the Natives. The relation may be genuinely poor and ill-fed and ill-favoured, but his clan is his passport. A wonderful fragrance of neighbourliness is thrown into all the outward converse

of life amongst the Natives by this invariable habit
of seeking links. If neither blood nor affinity can
produce a link, then simple friendliness of heart must
supply the want. If you can do nothing else, at least
you can shake out of your pouch a few crumbs of
tobacco, and by so doing you at once earn a title of
friendship. You are *Bawo* (my father) or *Mtwan' am*
(my child).

When I was scribbling these words I had off-saddled
my horse in the course of a long ride. I was sitting by
the side of a path looking over wide stretches of
veld. Two " red " Natives came riding along the path
on horseback. One of them was riding a mare, and
the foal, nearly a two-year-old, was running behind
according to the custom of the country. The foal
began to take an interest in my horse and to graze
alongside of it. The man who was riding the mother
did not at first notice this, so I went to the rescue,
and began to drive the foal after him. He turned
and saw what I was doing, " Mnumzetu undincedile,"
he said. I had earned the title of fellowship. I
belonged to the family, I was the " owner of the kraal,"
because I had shown *ubuntu*. The man would readily
and instinctively have done for me what I did for him,
but the surprise of it was that a white man should do
if for a Native. Even as I was writing another " red "
Native came along on foot. We chatted, and I found
that he had come from far. I was eating some break-
fast and I broke the bread in two pieces to share it
with the stranger. *Bawo!* (my father), he said. I had
earned the title of "father" because I shared a piece
of bread. The man would, without hesitation, have
shared his food with a stranger, but the wonder was
that a white man should share with a Native. It was
ubuntu, and white folk are generally lacking in *ubuntu*.
That is the pity of it. Nothing in the world can atone

for the lack of *ubuntu*. It is the crucial test by which, more and more, manhood is tried. Without it a man may be wealthy, successful, influential, but he will have cast away the dignity of human nature. He is not a neighbour. It is not on account of material advantage that a Native seeks to establish links with others. He is essentially sociable, and nothing is dearer to him than *ubuncoko* (chatting). What is the use of saying that you are a friend if you are not willing to spend a few minutes—hours, perhaps—in pleasant conversation? The questioning of the stranger, so irritating and unwelcome to the white man, is the essence of politeness in the Native. To the white man it is bad manners to question a stranger about his own concerns. To the Native it would be bad manners not to question him. His concerns are *not* private just because he is not really a stranger ; he is a member of the human family. To betray indifference to his concerns is to deny interest in him. It belongs only to the sorcerer and the thief to be reserved and secretive and to hide their concerns. They have very good reasons for so doing. They are " playing their own game " and not *the* game. They are essentially the individualists. They are anti-social, and everything anti-social is abomination to the Native. In all these ways and in many others the Native shows that an *umntu* (person) must be a neighbour.

As I think over the corporal acts of mercy I find that the primitive Native has, in this respect, nothing to learn. He claims no credit for it. *Of course* he lays aside his own business to go to bury his third cousin. *Of course* if he hears that some distant relation is sick he goes off to visit him. *Of course* he shares the last food in his kraal with the stranger who comes to see him. All this is just *ubuntu*.

Not that the Natives are free from the sins against
neighbourliness. On the contrary, these are much in
evidence. They speak evil of one another, they
quarrel, they fight, they suspect one another of sorcery,
they are far too ready to engage their neighbour in
lawsuits, they do not respect the sanctity of the
marriage tie. In all these ways they offend against
the golden law of charity. Yet it is hardly open to
question, that the outstanding quality of the people
is neighbourliness.

And is it not true that in all these ways the primitive
Native is not far from the Kingdom of Heaven ?

Such was the atmosphere of the " Ancient Kraal,"
and it is out of such an atmosphere that the Native
steps when he knocks, as a postulant, at the door of
the " New Kraal."

The first word that he learns as he steps over the
threshold is *Bawo wetu*—" Our Father." It is a word
which not only stamps all the good fellowship of life
with a divine sanction, it also teaches that every
member of the " New Kraal " who would have God
for Father must have man for brother.

As he learns the mysteries of the " New Kraal,"
he finds that God is revealed in Jesus Christ, not only
as Creator, but also as *neighbour*. He learns that the
new tribe has no limits of race narrower than humanity,
and, if he would have the neighbourly succour of Jesus
Christ for himself, he must himself be a neighbour
to all.

Perhaps he does not find this at all in fact, but
the ideal is enshrined in the faith and teaching of the
" New Kraal." Perhaps he goes to work in European
towns and villages amongst those who belong nominally
to the Fold, and is brought up against strange and
unhappy contradictions. Perhaps on the Mission
Station itself, amongst those who shared in his welcome

into the "New Kraal," he finds unbrotherliness and unneighbourliness far worse and more culpable than anything he experienced in the "Ancient Kraal." But, if his faith can withstand such rude shocks, if he can continually turn from the contradictions of the wayward to the attestations of the steadfast, he will find the fellowship of the "Ancient Kraal" again, re-born, in the charity of the new.

"She [the Church] is so divinely adjusted to it [the world] that nothing can it truly need but she shall automatically respond : the mere craving of the world's infant lips suffices to draw from her maternal and ever-yielding bosom the milk." *

Holy Church, the convert finds, carries the old questions, *Uvela pi? Uya pi?* † beyond the view of the "Ancient Kraal," and asks the new-born convert to remember that it is from out of the creative Hands of God that he comes, that it is by the living Way that he travels, and that it is to the Eternal Kraal not made with hands that he is going.

When our Lord was asked for a definition of a neighbour He made His appeal to *ubuntu* (humanity). The Priest and the Levite of the parable are clearly shown to have cast away the dignity of manhood. The Good Samaritan is arrayed for all time in that dignity. Our Lord Himself is seen to be *the neighbour* in a double capacity. He both stoops down to relieve the needs of a wounded humanity, and identifies Himself with every suppliant—"inasmuch as ye did it unto one of these, ye did it unto Me."

Ubuntu is then the obvious finger-post pointing to the golden goal of the love which was born in the world on the Day of Pentecost. The Native is to be

---

* *Prose Works of Francis Thompson*, p. 271.
† Where are you coming from ? Where are you going ?

UVELA PI? UYA PI?

"HE GOES OFF TO EAT THE MEAT OF THE CARCASE."

facing p. 30.

"HE LIVES IN TODAY"

facing p. 31

born again into the new clan, and there is to find a
new *ubuntu*—the love which is shed abroad in our
hearts by the Holy Spirit.

To present the Native with an individualistic Gospel
is to run clean contrary to all that is best in his own
tradition. To invite him to membership in a Church
in which the generous spirit of fellowship is dead or
dormant is to kill the very instincts of religion in his
heart. To offer him within the Church a back seat,
where he may admire the virtues of the superior race,
is to quench the live coal of the Holy Spirit in his soul.
Surely to us who are heirs of a great Christian civilisation St. Paul writes, " For I say, through the grace
given unto me, to every man that is among you, not
to think of himself more highly than he ought to think,
but to think soberly, according as God hath dealt
to every man the measure of faith. For as we have
many members in one body and all members have not
the same office : So we, being many, are one body
in Christ, and every one members one of another "
(Rom. xii. 3–5).

CHAPTER IV

TO-DAY AND TO-MORROW (*NAMHLANJE : NGOMSO*)

" We all get exhausted in the terrible contest between the European worker who bears the responsibility and is always in a hurry and the child of nature who does not know what responsibility is and is never in a hurry."

" Unborn To-morrow, and dead Yesterday,
Why fret about them, if To-day be sweet ? "

THERE are few words so common amongst our Native people in South Africa as *Ngomso* (to-morrow). This is not because the Native thinks and plans a great deal for the morrow. It would be far more true to say of the primitive Native that he neither thinks nor plans at all for it. He lives in to-day.

In Native life the shadow of to-morrow is very seldom allowed to fall upon the sunshine of to-day. But, more than that, to-morrow is a most convenient grave into which all unwelcome calls upon effort and exertion may be decently interred.

Let us take the former thought first. The shadow of to-morrow is very seldom allowed to fall upon the sunshine of to-day. That is truly good, with certain qualifications. Up to a certain point the Evangelical law against over-anxiety has found a congenial home amongst the Natives who have never even heard of the Giver of that law. Such anxiety is not only wrong, it is *bad form*. It presents itself largely as something individualistic and unsocial. No man has any right to mope, chiefly because he is a member of a community. Cheerfulness is primarily a social virtue, or duty. Anxiety, moping and worry, are sins of selfishness, and are on a par with such grave offences as eating in private, and even with the mortal sin of grudging.

If the trouble is a real and present one, then it is a matter not for the individual merely, but for the community. This is delightfully illustrated by a phrase used when the sacrificial meal is being eaten. When some have finished before others they say, " Oh, let us join with you. We see you are in *trouble*." If a man is in trouble it is a public concern—something to be shared. He may not have private troubles any more than he may have private food.

The shadow of to-morrow may only be valid reason for sorrow when it belongs to the whole community, and even then it is rarely allowed to darken the sunshine of to-day.

A man who is over-anxious is generally felt to be one who is separating himself from the community, and one of the most characteristic of Xosa proverbs is that " a bird builds its nest with the feathers of another bird " (*i.e.* a man cannot build his house by himself).

It is quite true that community of interest has its limits, and the limits are strongly defined in ownership. It is curious that the worst malefactors amongst the Natives are the man who challenges the law of ownership by thieving and the man who abuses the law of ownership by grudging.

The stingy man and the thief are both outside the pale, and worthy of excommunication.

The man who is over-anxious is too much wrapped

up in his own interests. He throws the shadow of
to-morrow upon the sunshine of to-day. But the
sunshine belongs to the community, and not to the
individual.

It is above all things necessary in Native life that
a man should be a good citizen—a member of a
community. His morality, like that of a Greek, is
summed up in the word πολιτεύεσθαι. He has to
be a good citizen, first in reference to the Chief to
whom he belongs; secondly, in reference to his elders
whose child he is; and thirdly, in reference to his
neighbours amongst whom he lives.

Even if the dread disease of East Coast fever reaches
his herd of cattle—the sum total of his wealth—he
must not let the shadow of to-morrow darken the
sunshine of to-day. He comes to the trading store
smiling, and haggles over the price of the hides which
have been brought on the heads of his wives. He
fills his pipe with the tobacco which he has begged as
discount on the bargain, and then he goes off to eat
the meat of the carcase with his friends. Has he
not got meat in abundance, and has he not got tobacco?
What more can he want? His "estate" is quite
a royal one. Even if this is the very last beast in the
kraal he has no right to anticipate the difficulties of
to-morrow.

Was there ever any one with such an amazing fund
of natural cheerfulness as this dark-skinned dweller
on the veld?

It is the *umlungu* (white man) who is the flagrant
transgressor of this great commandment of Native
life. But then what can one expect of an *umlungu*!
Poor man, he is greatly to be pitied. He has never
been properly brought up. He has not learnt the
very elements of "good form." Almost everything
he does infringes the law of good citizenship. Perhaps

it is hardly to be expected that any one so badly brought up should share his food with a man of dark skin, but, apparently, he does not even share his food with a man of his own colour. He goes to an hotel where he buys his food, and he buys his drink !

Of course a man like that is sure to be wrapped up in his own interests. He is sure to worry and be anxious about his own concerns. He is sure to let the shadow of to-morrow darken the sunshine of to-day.

Amongst *abelungu* (white folk) each one, of course, has his *own* patch of sunshine. So perhaps it does not matter so much. The white man builds walls round his house and walls round his garden, so probably he will soon build walls round his own private stock of sunshine !

But let us look a little further into this matter. Amongst the Native people the morrow is a most convenient grave into which all the unwelcome calls upon effort and exertion may be happily buried. Here, again, it is the *umlungu* (white man) who offends so grievously against good form. Really the white man is a most unreasonable person. He is not con- tent with making his own life miserable, he will insist on making the lives of other people miserable too. With all possible politeness you tell him that you will make his bricks for him *to-morrow*, and, as likely as not, he works himself up into a passion and tells you that unless you will begin at this very moment you can make yourself scarce ! Again, you tell the white man at the trading store in the most friendly way possible that you will settle your account *to-morrow*, and, immediately, before the words are fairly out of your mouth, he begins to talk about a lawyer's letter of demand !

The truth is, the white man has an altogether exaggerated estimate of to-day. Knowing that he

has such a very slight acquaintance with " good form "
you try to humour him, but it is an exceedingly difficult
job. And yet the white man tells you that he believes
in *u-Tixo* (God), and that God cares for him ! Really
the white man is the most incomprehensible person !
Even the *abafundisi* (missionaries) are very much
to blame in this matter. It is true that in many
things they are not like other *abelungu* (white men),
but they, too, are extraordinarily lacking in faith.
If they are building a church or a school they worry
themselves to such a degree that they almost succeed
in making some foolish Natives worry too.

It is always *to-day*. The headman must call the
meeting about the building *to-day*. If he ventures to
talk about *to-morrow* the Mfundisi gets positively hot.
And now, when the builder is engaged, he must begin
to cut the sods *to-day*. The Mfundisi says that
to-morrow the ground will be too dry to cut sods.
And then, when the walls are built, the roof must
be put on *to-day*. Really such impatience is quite
indecent ! If you venture to say that you will begin
to-morrow, he will tell you that the rain is coming
to-morrow and that it will bring down the walls !

You, of course, are very glad to hear that the
rain is coming to-morrow. You are longing for rain,
and *U-Mfundisi* ought to know better than any one
when the rain is coming. You go home and tell
your friends what *U-Mfundisi* has said, and they
are all glad. Unfortunately the next day it is as
dry as ever, and the people begin to lose faith in
U-Mfundisi.

Yes, the white man may be very clever, and he
may do many wonderful things, but he has not yet
learnt that " sufficient unto the day is the evil thereof,"
and that the really wise man defers to *to-morrow* the
thing which is too difficult for him to do *to-day !*

CHAPTER V

THE RELIGION OF THE HEARTH
(" *BIKELA AMAZIKO* ")

"In proportion as he [the Native] becomes familiar with the higher moral ideas of the religion of Jesus he finds utterance for something in himself that has hitherto been dumb."

THIS phrase, "*Bikela amaziko*," is one which brings us close to the very heart of the Bantu people. Perhaps no other single phrase in Xosa does more to bridge over the gulf which separates the Bantu from the great peoples of the past.

The words may be translated quite simply as a direction to convey a message to the various members of a certain family, or to the families of a certain clan, or to the clans of a certain tribe. I am chiefly concerned with the words as applying to the members of a family.

Possibly some member of the family is seriously ill. An important decision has to be made. A sacrifice, perhaps, has to be offered. A matter of such moment does not just concern the father, mother, brothers and sisters who are living in the family kraal. It concerns the grandparents, the uncles, the married daughters, etc. All must be told.

The word used for such relatives, *amaziko*, is of peculiar interest. It means the hearth, but it is in the plural, and perhaps the nearest translation would be, " All who belong to the hearth."

37

What is this hearth ?   Actually it is a little circle in the centre of the mud floor of the hut, outlined by a raised moulding of mud, upon which day by day the fire is laid.

But, in this phrase, this very simple hearth becomes the symbol of a great deal that is of essential value. It symbolises the great reality of one family—the bond of the family, the authority and permanence of the family.

It is true that, at any rate in these days, the cattle kraal rather than the hearth is the *sacred* place and the symbol of the family.   As has been pointed out to me by a friendly critic of this paper, the removal of a village or its burning in war is nothing to the loss of cattle, and their loss is not the mere loss of property— it is a sentimental, religious loss.   The *ubulungu*, or sacrificial cattle, are lost.

Yet there must be a peculiar significance in the fact that all who belong to the family are known as *amaziko*, those who are near the hearth.   Even if the word were just a picturesque figure, the force of the figure must depend upon something solid behind, something which has kindled the imagination and touched the affections of the people.   *Iziko*, the hearth, must have stood for something of real value.

Even such a picturesque phrase as " playing the game " would mean little to Englishmen if it were not that " the game " is taken very seriously and forms a real feature in our national characteristics.

It may be that the hearth is linked in thought to the cattle kraal as representing in symbol the home and the unity of the family.   Or it may be that the use of the word " hearth " to represent the family comes from earlier times when the hearth possessed more sacred significance.

In this connection it is striking to notice that, in

certain clans of the Ama-Tonga, the two ancestors
of mankind are called by names which mean, "One
who brought a glowing cinder in a shell," and "One
who grinds vegetables." The former, the male, is
the originator of fire ; the latter, the female, uses the
fire for cooking. It would seem that the primal
ancestor of the race, according to this view, was the
creator of the hearth. He kindled fire, and round
the hearth upon which that fire was kindled the human
family gathers.

But we must return to the hearth of our Bantu
family. There is, as we said, some serious calamity.
A member of the family is sick, and therefore all the
members of the family are sick. The Bantu Natives
need not be told that if one member suffer all the
members suffer with it. If you meet one of a family
to which a sick man belongs, and make the usual
inquiry after his health, he will say, "I am not well
by reason of so-and-so." He himself is perfectly
well, but he is a member of a family that is sick.
Because one is sick, all are sick.

So the word goes forth, "*Bikela amaziko*"—go
and tell all who belong to the hearth. Omit no one.
Even to-day, when some of the family may be away
at Johannesburg working in underground mines, they
too must be informed. Some one must write to tell
them of the family misfortune. Then the members
of the family—all who belong to the hearth—collect
together.

By this time, perhaps, the witch doctor has already
declared that this is not a sickness due to the wiles of
sorcery, but is on account of the displeasure of the
ancestors, and that a sacrifice is required.

Here we reach a further point in the meaning of
amaziko. It is not the living only who belong to the
hearth, but the ancestors too. And the ancestors

are not far distant—they have an immediate influence upon the living members of the family. When those who belong to the hearth are all gathered together the departed are also present.

The victim of the sacrifice is stabbed, and the first thing to be done is to give to these departed members of the family their share. Certain portions of the fat are taken and consumed by fire.

Thus we get a picture of the family with its strong bond of union—a bond which unites not only those who are in the flesh, but even the spirits of the ancestors. They are all *amaziko :* they belong to the hearth.

Speaking of this strong family bond, Bishop Key once wrote, "The Pondomisi youth as he came to manhood looked forward to become a member of his family. . . . If he does wrong his father and his brothers will pay for him ; if his rights are attacked they will see him righted ; if he is hungry they will give him food ; if he is to be married they will fetch his wife home, and pay dowry for her. He and they are one."

Nothing is more abhorrent to the Bantu Native than the cutting asunder, the schism, of the family bond. As we have already seen, even death itself is not regarded as destructive of that bond.

There are, however, two forms of excommunication from the hearth, one of which is primitive and ancient, while the other is modern, and results from contact with European civilisation.

According to the ancient order, if a member of a family were to disgrace the family name, and were to reject all the warnings and persuasions of elders, he was at length formally and solemnly excommunicated by his father in the presence of the *amaziko*—all who belong to the hearth. The ritual act proper to this ceremony in some tribes is peculiar. A little blood

from the ear of a dog was dropped into a small vessel
containing milk, and the father of the person to be
excommunicated would take a mouthful of this and
then spit it out. It would then be said, "U-yise
umhlambile unyana wake"—"The father has cast
off his son."

The modern schism of the family bond to which
I referred should perhaps be called self-excommunica-
tion, and it is becoming terribly common. You may
meet a Native man whom you have not seen for years,
and you ask after his son; *utshipile* is the answer.
The word is entirely of recent date, but every one
knows what it means. It means that some five, or
six, or seven years ago, or even more, the young man
went off to one of the great centres of "civilisation."
He bound himself to work for six months, and, when
he first went away, he comforted his relations by
assuring them that he would soon send money to pay
the family debts, and that the six months would quickly
pass. Letters come from the lad to his home during
the first two or three months, and then there is silence.
The six months pass, and he does not return. Letters
are written, but they are not answered. Other men
from the same neighbourhood come back from the
mines, and they say that they have seen the young
man, but their information is very scanty. Two or
three years elapse, and then the parents meet all
inquiry about their son by this one sad, pathetic
word, *utshipile*—he has excommunicated himself from
the family hearth.

If the young man in question happens to be the
eldest son, and if his father dies while he is in the
"far country," everything in the real inward life of
that family seems to come to an end. The family
has no head, no bond of union, and the younger sons
spend much time, energy, and money in efforts to get

back to the home one who, for the good of the family, had better, from that point of view, never return. The isolation of the individual seems to be contrary to the deepest and most religious instincts of the Bantu Native. No single person should be homeless— unconnected with a hearth.

But the Bantu Native looked beyond the hearth, with all that it signified, to the clan, and beyond the clan to the tribe. Did he look beyond the tribe to the claims of a common humanity ? I think there is evidence that he did so. It is true that, in days of inter-tribal warfare, tribe would prey upon tribe, but there was probably the continual consciousness that warfare broke links which were ordained to bind, and that those links might yet be forged anew. As was said above, the primal ancestor of the race was some-times conceived of as the creator of a hearth. He kindled a fire, and round the hearth upon which that fire was kindled the human family was intended to gather.

It ought not to be difficult for the Native to con-ceive of Babel as the destruction of the primal hearth. The thoughtful convert to Christianity readily sees the selfish and destructive tendencies of excessive racialism and nationalism. He is prepared to recognise Pentecost as the new creation—the restoration of a hearth for the world-wide family. The fire of the Holy Ghost was then kindled and became the centre of the new family in which there is to be " neither bond nor free, neither Jew nor Gentile."

In the Christian sense *bikela amaziko* might well be applied to the calling of an Ecumenical Council to be gathered round the " hearth," upon which is kindled the fire of the Holy Spirit.

Locally the words might apply to the summoning of a Synod to gather round the Bishop of a Diocese at the Cathedral which represents the family hearth. But, far beyond any application which belongs to time and space, is the thought that these words reach on forward to the gathering together of the " great multitude which no man could number, of all nations, and kindreds, and people, and tongues," which " stood before the Lamb, clothed with white robes, and palms in their hands ; and cried with a loud voice, saying, Salvation to our God which sitteth upon the throne, and unto the Lamb." These are the *amaziko*—they belong to that hearth of which it is said that " the glory of the Lord did lighten it, and the Lamb is the light thereof."

In that day all the dreams and hopes of an universal hearth will find their fulfilment ; the fellowship which looks so impossible to-day will be realised. The Fatherhood of God will at last be seen manifested in the brotherhood of man.

CHAPTER VI

THE UNFINISHED HOME

SONAMZI had chosen a beautiful spot for his future home. It was at the extreme end of a ridge which gradually sloped back until it lost itself in the broad sides of the Kwanca Mountain. The ridge ended rather abruptly, and, just below it, hemmed in by a slow-flowing stream, was a flat piece of land measuring a few acres. At this flat piece of land Sonamzi was now looking. He had been cutting sods in the virgin veld, and he stood there leaning on his spade. That piece of land below, as yet untouched by the plough, opened up to him visions of the future.

Hitherto he had ploughed for his father, hoed for his father, and reaped for his father. Soon he was going, for the first time, to plough for himself—and for another. He looked forward from the ploughing to the reaping, and from the reaping to the quiet evenings in his own home when the cooking-pot would be on the fire, and, under the lid, he would catch sight of the firstfruits of his own land.

Then his eyes wandered to the steep sides of the kopje across the stream where, amidst the half-hidden rocks, the goats from a neighbouring kraal were nibbling the sweet grass. It did not require a very vivid imagination to picture another little flock feeding alongside of that one. Already he owned a few, and the increase was only a matter of time. The thought of the goats at once suggested the need of a kraal in which they would be sheltered at night, and Sonamzi began to measure with his eye a space in front of the hut he had begun to build.

Yes! a kraal would do very well there, and it would be quite easy to get the *amahlahla* (branches) from the small forest which lay half hidden in a depression on the side of the ridge. A bright look came into the boy's dark face as he caught sight of a distant kraal above the forest. Perhaps, amongst the people sitting about that kraal, he may have seen Tandiwe who, in less than a month, was to be his wife.

He had done enough work for that day. Already the walls of his hut were nearly five feet above the ground, and two more rows of sods would complete them. Shouldering his spade, Sonamzi turned off up the ridge. In places he noticed that quite a path had been worn in the veld from his frequent journeys, and he smiled as he thought that that path would soon be well defined and would be known as " the path to Sonamzi's kraal."

Again, on the following day, Sonamzi was at the end of the ridge. He had begun to lay the sods of the last row but one. But to-day his face is clouded. All the spring seems to have gone out of his movements, and soon he throws aside his spade, and, sitting down, he buries his face between his knees.

While he is sitting there a man who has climbed up the steep end of the ridge comes up to him.

" *Molo* (good day), Sonamzi."

" *Ewe* " (yes), is the answer.

" When will you finish your hut ? "

" In a few days."

" Why are you not working now ? "

" I don't know."

" Are you not well ? "

" Yes, I am well."

This was not strictly true, for Sonamzi was not well. When he went home on the previous day he had left his spade at his father's kraal, and then he had gone to see Tandiwe. Tandiwe was sitting with her back towards him as he approached, and he had walked lightly on purpose to surprise the look of welcome in her eyes as he came up. She was talking to another girl, and Sonamzi could hear that the conversation was continually interrupted by Tandiwe's cough. As he came up she had a particularly violent fit of coughing which shook her whole body. This is why Sonamzi was not well. This cough of Tandiwe's troubled him sorely. He remembered that her elder sister, who died two years ago, previously had had a cough like that. Tandiwe had always said before that she was getting better, and that the medicine was doing her good, but now, as he looked into her large sunken eyes, he knew that her hopes were over-sanguine.

He had not cut any more sods that day, and he went home while the sun was still high. As usual he left his spade in his father's hut, and was about to walk over to Tandiwe's kraal.

" Where are you going to, my son ? " said a woman sitting outside the hut.

" I am going to see Tandiwe."

" She is not at home."

" Where has she gone to ? "

" She has gone to the Hospital at the Mission."

" When will she return ? "

" I do not know ; sit down, my son, and I will tell you more."

*   *   *   *   *

A few months later, when I crossed the stream of the Kwanca Mountain, the walls of Sonamzi's hut were still standing, although the summer rains had made a breach in the back, and the last row of sods had never been added. I could see no trace of the path in the veld, which was to lead to "Sonamzi's kraal."

CHAPTER VII

WITCHCRAFT

"Il ne faut jamais oublier quand on étudie la mentalité des noirs que, pour eux, le monde des esprits est très proche."

PEOPLE ask sometimes if the belief in witchcraft is dying out amongst the people—the heathen— of this country. It is difficult to answer this question, as the people are so exceedingly reticent on this subject. I doubt if even our Christian people know the full extent of the practice of "witchcraft." If they do, they are exceedingly shy of speaking to us about it. I often wonder about this reticence. To some extent I expect it implies lingering belief and an unconscious dread of speaking about such matters, especially to "unbelievers" like ourselves. Here is a case of witchcraft which happened recently quite close to St. Cuthbert's amongst the heathen.

A heathen man was ill for some time, and his illness refused to yield to ordinary treatment. Perhaps we should not be surprised at this if we knew what "ordinary treatment" means amongst the Natives. Very probably an *ixwele* (herbalist) had been called in. Although such a man professes to treat disease by herbs, he knows that his herbs will carry much more "suggestion" if there is also some appeal to the mystery of magic. In this case both medicine and magic seem to

48

have failed. Very probably the herbalist may also have offered a goat in sacrifice to propitiate the offended ancestors. Finally, some of the relatives went off to a "witch doctor" in Pondoland. This "doctor" is known as *igqira*, which by common consent is the name also given to the ordinary European practitioner. In this case the "doctor" was a woman, and we are told that on this occasion her fee was £1. It is not easy for English folk to remember that such a person is very highly regarded by the Native people. She is a protector of society against the wiles of sorcerers. The sorcerer is the individualist who uses occult powers for his own private ends, and is a danger to the welfare of the people generally.

The witch doctor is a duly qualified person who is *twasile*. We should translate this last word, perhaps, as "one who has taken a diploma in medicine." Such a person is, in a sense, an "arm of the law," and is regarded in something the same way as we might regard the superior detective, or policeman, or even magistrate. He, or she, is supposed to be on the side of "righteousness," but he has not obtained his power by merely natural means. There has been a period of initiation into the mysteries, during which he has held communication with the unseen world. It is strange to me that this profession, which ranks so high, should be open to women. Women are not supposed to have any "political" rights, and yet they can wield enormous power as "witch doctors." In this case the "lady doctor" held her court. She rigged herself out, no doubt, in the full paraphernalia of her office, including the skins of wild animals. Then she would use all the devices known to the trade to hypnotize the audience. She gradually throws herself into a strange frenzy, her whole body breaking out into perspiration owing to the violence of her

contortions. At last she would ask them to " agree,"
and this stage of the proceedings gives its name to the
whole process of inquiry—*ukuvumisa* (literally, to make
to agree). " We agree," the inquirers say. The
witch doctor leads them on from stage to stage, and
finally tells them, with their " agreement," that the
sickness is caused by a person. The person in this
case was said to be a woman. She would tell no more,
and the inquirers go home with the news. The
verdict is absolutely accepted, but it is unsatisfactory.
The family conclave feels that they must go further
and find out who the woman is. Off they go to another
witch doctor, and they pay her 11s. 6d. She is more
compliant than the first, and tells them that the
sorcerer who is causing the illness is the wife of the
sick man. Home they go and report the result.
The poor wife receives the news, accepts it, and
swallows a dose of arsenical sheep-dip, and dies. She
is proved to be a *sorcerer*, and she cannot bear the
reproach.

It is so strange that the Xosa word for " sorcerer "
only differs by one letter from the word for " witch
doctor," who is the direct antithesis to the sorcerer.
The enemy of society (the sorcerer) is *igqwira*. The
protector of society is *igqira*. When the poor woman
was asked by her friends, before she took the poison,
if she accepted the word of the witch doctor, she
assented, and even said, " Why should not I believe it,
when this is my second husband, and both have been
ill ? "

What a lot of questions it suggests ! Did the poor
" sorcerer "—or " sorceress "—really believe that she
was causing her husband's death ? If so, did she
believe that she did it consciously and of malignant
purpose, or did she believe that she did it in her sleep,
when she was scarcely responsible ? And the witch

doctors, did they really believe in themselves and their own skill and their own verdicts? Or were they merely trading upon superstitions? And were these superstitions recognised as such?

It is very difficult to answer these questions. My impression is that the *gqira* (witch doctor) himself believes, in common with the great majority of the people, that sorcery is a real thing and a common thing. They believe, I suppose, that hatred and jealousy and envy can find other than open and "honest" channels by which to injure the person against whom they are directed. Perhaps we should almost say the same. Should we not say that if the evil spirit of hatred and envy were nursed in secret until it became an obsession, it would almost inevitably communicate itself to the injury of others?

The Native would, of course, say more than that. He would say that the way by which such an evil spirit communicated itself would be by unlawful, forbidden and evil practices of dark mysterious science. He would say that the "sorcerer" had possessed himself of the tooth or a few hairs of the victim of his displeasure, and that by means of these he was reaching and injuring their lawful owner. Such a person must be met and fought on his own ground. If he uses magic, then magic must be employed against him. If he learns secrets from the complaisant spirits of the unseen world, he must be conquered by one who has similar access to that unseen world.

With such beliefs you can imagine what terrible temptations sickness may bring even to a good Christian. It is not easy to uproot such beliefs, but when health and strength are normal they are easily put away. It is when sickness robs its victim of normal control that old beliefs come whispering at the door. But the evil of such a belief is infinite. It robs life of its confidence and sows seeds of suspicion and distrust and fear and revenge in the minds of the people. In the great majority of cases, where the verdict of the witch doctor falls upon a supposed sorcerer there is not even proof of enmity.

CHAPTER VIII

THE WITCH DOCTOR

I WAS riding one day, and as I neared the top of the ascent, at quite the most beautiful spot in the whole ride, I met a strange procession coming down the path. It would almost be correct to call it a *religious* procession, and suddenly I seemed to see what it might have been had the religion been Christianity. I seemed to see a stately Abbess mounted on a horse, accompanied by some of her nuns and a few novices. It might have been St. Theresa herself going to visit one of her Foundations. But the religion was not Christianity—it was *Primitive*, and my " Abbess " was an *igqirakazi*—commonly called, in the vulgar tongue, witch doctor. It was a remarkable sight, and I wished for a skilled artist to reproduce the scene. Could it be reproduced exactly at the British Empire Exhibition it would undoubtedly create a sensation.

First of all came (on foot) a Native girl, not in any way differentiated from her sisters in any of the surrounding kraals. In my own mind I thought of her as still a " postulant " craving admission in the fellowship of witch doctors. Behind her came several girls and women who were obviously " novices." They had discarded, as is the custom, all red clay and were " clothed " in the habit of the Order—white blankets. Probably they were at different stages of

53

the novitiate, as one or two were allowed to wear some
of the distinctive ornaments of the profession. Then
came two men, on foot, who were just attendants or
escort. But the outstanding figure was the " Abbess "
sitting with much dignity astride on her horse. She
was rigged out in all the paraphernalia of the profession. The dominant colour was white, for she too
wore white blankets, but the beadwork, which clustered
round her neck and was attached in various ways to
her blankets, was rich in colour and, withal, of excellent
harmony. On her head she wore a cap made of a
monkey-skin, and springing out of this were two tall
white feathers plucked, perhaps, from a large hawk.
The tails of two (I think there were two) monkey-
skins hung down her neck at the back rather like the
tails of a bishop's mitre. It would not have been
becoming of me to note too carefully all the details,
but I have no doubt that there were dried gall bladders
given as fees for successful cases, and horns filled
with powdered roots and snakes' skins and various
" tools of the trade."

I would willingly have asked many questions.
In fact, I should like to have asked the " Abbess " of
her courtesy to dismount and give me the favour of
a little conversation, but I could see and feel that my
presence gave cause for some uneasiness. They knew
who I was and were not disposed to answer questions.
They said merely that they were on an errand of
" business." I wished I could make the " Abbess "
understand that my interest was not a mocking one,
nor exactly hostile, but absolutely serious. We shall
never understand the meaning of witchcraft and its
place in the mental life of the people until we take
it seriously, and until we realise that it touches some
of the deepest as well as some of the darkest feelings
of the Native heart. I felt that my " Abbess " was

a woman of power. Her face and speech both showed
intelligence. No doubt she had succeeded in establishing herself in her position by real power of mind and
character. She was both doctor and priestess in one,
and, in the Native mind, the two ideas are never
far distant from one another. If one could separate
the *woman* from her methods, one would probably
find something of the psycho-analyst, with a shrewd
insight into mental processes, an intelligence deliberately trained to read riddles, and perhaps a spiritual
as opposed to a materialistic reading of the universe.

I expect she was an *igqira lokuvumisa* (doctor for
the purpose of divination), and perhaps at that very
moment she was going to preside at some gathering
called for that purpose. Her work would not be
accomplished in the quiet, cool, self-possessed manner
of the Harley Street physician. In his case quiet-
ness of manner and a certain assurance are aids to
his power of suggestion and persuasion. But my
"Abbess" has to deal with very different clients,
and she knows perfectly well that her influence depends
largely upon the mystery of her communications, and
upon the frenzied "ecstasy" with which they are
communicated. In her own mind she believes,
perhaps as fully as the Harley Street physician, that
she is a benefactor and protector of society. She is
out to combat the wickedness and evil machinations
of sorcerers and malignant spirits.

Professor Willoughby, in his recently published
book on the Bantu,* suggests that a sorcerer is only a
quack, as opposed to a professional, witch doctor. I
cannot think that this is correct. There is actually
such a thing as a "quack witch doctor," with a
recognised name as such. But the sorcerer, who may,

* " Race Problems in the New Africa " (1923):

of course, be perfectly innocent of any offence at all, is in the minds of the people the person who is using secret and magical powers for personal and selfish ends and from bad and sinister motives.

I believe that, on the whole, my " Abbess " is probably sincere in her belief that she has powers, derived from unseen beings and ancestral spirits wherewith to overthrow the dangerous malignity of sorcerers and vengeful spirits.

PART III

THE NEW FELLOWSHIP

CHAPTER IX

FELLOWSHIP IN THE HOME
(*XALISWA MAKUBONE*)

"**W**ELL, Nellie, why did you run away from school?" "Bendikumbula ikaya" ("I remembered home") was the perfectly simple answer of a young Native girl of about twelve years old. To her it was a perfectly reasonable and sufficient answer. Was it not good to "remember home"? Was it not absolutely dutiful, and right, and proper, to "remember home"? Would it not be absolutely wrong and unpardonable not to "remember home"?

That was many years ago. To-day little girls have come to realise that white people do not consider *that* reason a sufficient one for leaving school, and now, too often, the answer lacks its ancient simplicity. To-day, after the school has dragged on for a good many weeks, it is astonishing to find how frequently the relatives of the children are afflicted with serious illness. Domestic servants, too, have a most inconvenient number of near relations who suffer from frequently recurring illness.

It would no doubt be easier for us to ignore this tendency to " remember home," but to do this ruthlessly would be to strike a blow at what is really one of the best influences of Native life.

During the last few years we have begun to find that some of our young men who go away to the mines, leaving wife and family behind them, do not return. Little by little they have ceased writing and sending any money to their relatives, until at last there is complete silence. After making fruitless endeavours to discover the whereabouts of the wanderer, we are obliged to wait patiently until there is " a mighty famine in that land " and he begins " to be in want." It is then that he may begin " to come to himself " and to remember home. It is not difficult to imagine how such a craving comes into the heart of the poor prodigal.

A picture comes before me of a gang of Native men engaged in pushing loaded trucks of a goods train along the line. It was not at any time a very cheering kind of work ; but with a fierce tropical sun overhead, and with an impatient overseer armed with a formidable *sjambok* (strip of rhinoceros hide) behind, it was not a job calculated to increase a man's self-respect.

Think of one of that gang of Native labourers, an ignorant, heathen man, as he returns to his own home on the veld. The European clothes which he donned in respect for his masters are soon laid aside in favour of the red-ochred blanket. But that is by no means the only, nor indeed the chief, change which results from his home-coming. In his own home he is no longer a serf : he is a citizen with real rights. People come to see him, and to talk with him, and to ask his advice. He has, in a material sense, " come to himself " ; he is a " son " and he is " found."

It is surely no wonder that many a wanderer as

he " remembers home " says within himself, " I will arise and go to my father."

On the veld there is no such thing as an orphanage ; not because the people are indifferent to suffering, but because they take care that there shall be no orphans, no *homeless* people. A lady once wrote to Bishop Key to ask if he would like her to open an orphanage for Native children in his diocese. His answer was, " There are no orphans." It is the glory of Native custom that this is true. It is true that there *is* a word for orphan in isi-Xosa, and the Native who wants to borrow money, or to secure free education, or charity of some sort, frequently urges the fact that he is an orphan. It may be perfectly true that his parents are dead : it may also be true that his elder brothers and even that his uncles and aunts are dead. But, even so, in *our* sense of the word he is not an orphan. According to Native custom there is always some one whom he can call " father," and some kraal which he can call " home."

Perhaps nothing would do more to condemn us and our civilisation in the eyes of the Natives than our " waifs and strays," our workhouses and all our homeless folk. " In a well-ordered society," the Native, heathen and Christian, would say, " there ought not to be such things as waifs and strays, orphans and homeless."

It is a real puzzle to a good Native to conceive of a society where such a thing is not only possible but permitted. To them the existence of a homeless person implies *fault*, and ultimately it must be the authorities, the rulers of that society, who are at fault. In the first instance it must either be the homeless person himself who is at fault or some one else who is neglecting obvious responsibilities.

I have been speaking of lessons learned, not in the

school of Christianity, but in that of the "Ancient Kraal." It is there that we find this strong attachment to home. At the same time, it must be admitted that this home-fellowship is often very roughly severed.

People who come from over the sea and journey through the Transkei have sometimes a wonderful way of idealising the life of the primitive Kafir. Away on ridges innumerable they see the huts of the people —these quiet, child-like people who live in great content upon the fruits of the earth and cherish the solid virtues of an untutored race, until they are disturbed by the intruding voice of the missionary. In those quiet homes men lie in graceful ease, sheltered from wild winds by the close-knit fence of the cattle kraal, discussing in grave and serious fashion the affairs of their new world politics ; while the women, trained from childhood in homes of domestic virtue, are busy preparing to supply the frugal needs of their lords and of their children.

It is a charming picture, and it has an element of truth. When we come to a close knowledge of heathen life we find, it is true, much that is good, much that must not be destroyed, much that needs to be brought into the regenerate life, but we find also that we come very close to " the snare of the enemy "—that ancient enemy of the Garden of Eden—" the noisome pestilence . . . the terror by night, and the arrow that flieth by day." As we come to close quarters with heathen life we find that we need that close-fitting armour which the Psalmist calls " the shadow of the Almighty."

In polygamy alone we have, of course, one very fruitful source of difficulty and discord. How wonderfully this is brought out for us in the old, old story of the home-life of the " Father of the faithful ! " " And Sarah saw the son of Hagar the Egyptian, which she

AN UP-COUNTRY STORE (A CORNER OF THE STOEP).

"THERE ARE NO ORPHANS."

facing p. 60.

GIRLS OF ST. CUTHBERT'S WEAVING SCHOOL.

facing p. 61.

had borne unto Abraham, mocking, whereupon she said unto Abraham, Cast out this bondwoman and her son : for the son of this bondwoman shall not be heir with my son, even with Isaac ! "

The history of Genesis repeats itself in numbers of Kafir kraals with sometimes even more disastrous results. I was sitting once in the visitors' room of the House of Correction in Roeland Street at Cape Town. It is a dull, dark room with bare furniture. I was talking to a quiet-looking Native woman who, less than three years before, had been convicted of a terrible crime.

" My name is Xaliswa," she said, " but when I was baptized *U-Mfundisi* [the priest] gave me the name of Sarah Jane."

It seems strange that any parents could give their child a name which means " burdened with care," but certainly the name came to fit its owner only too well, and I am glad that as she entered the fold of the Good Shepherd—the " New Kraal "—she received a new name.

Xaliswa began to speak of her home on the veld. " Does the Father know that country ? " " Yes ? Oh, that is good. *U-Mfundisi* who comes to give me my Communion is kind, but he cannot speak to me in isi-Xosa. He does not know my country. It is good of God to send me *U-Mfundisi* who knows my country."

Of course we did not say one word about the crime. I rejoiced to see the transforming power of grace and to know that the sin had been swept away in the living stream which flows from the Fountain which opened at Calvary. But how had it happened ?

Xaliswa's first husband died, leaving her with one little girl named Nonjinji. Then it was that her life began to be " burdened with care." According to the heathen custom of these parts, Xaliswa was now claimed to wife by Xala, her late husband's brother. As if her own name were not ominous enough, Xaliswa was now mated to one whose name was just the root-form of her own and meant " care."

If environment alone could have healed the wound in Xaliswa's heart, and could have brought peace and happiness into her life, I think her new home would have been all-sufficient. It happened, one day, that I was anxious to meet some friends who would, I knew, be obliged to cross the Ncambele River somewhere in that neighbourhood. I looked out for a vantage-point from which I might without difficulty keep my watch over many miles of the country. Although I did not know it at the time, I chose a spot within fifty yards of Xaliswa's new home. It was a winter day, bright and cloudless. The veld had been scorched by months of sun by day and nipped by heavy frost at night.

Far below me the cattle were grazing in the recently reaped lands, where the dry mealie stalks still offered attractive fare. Amongst the mealie lands the Ncambele River wandered at will, like a vagrant thread of blue in a carpet of yellow and brown and gold. Beyond the river were more mealie lands, more sun-browned veld, more ridges covered with kraals, and then came the beautiful mountains, still guarding with tenacious fidelity their rich treasures of forest.

God was speaking through it all, " for the invisible things of Him since the creation of the world are clearly seen, being perceived through the things that are made, even His everlasting power and divinity." But His voice did not reach the heart of Xaliswa through the forms and colours of created loveliness. It was not in the way of earthly content, but in the *via dolorosa* that she was destined to hear His Voice. The trouble was that Xala was already married, and his first wife did not regard this intruder with any favour.

If I had asked Xaliswa how she could account for the terrible tragedy which ultimately took place, I think she would just have said, with Sarah her namesake, "She 'mocked' me." Day by day, hour by hour, jealousy and hatred ripened. Recourse was, no doubt, had to friends who were learned in the "black art" by both the women. Charms and roots were equally unavailing. One day a very whirlwind of rage blinded poor Xaliswa to all consequences, and, seizing the axe used to chop the firewood, she quickly silenced for ever the taunting voice.

Then what happened?

Out on the veld we hardly know that morbid curiosity which invests a crime with a halo of distinction. In the presence of a terrible tragedy such as this it is felt that it becomes a man to be grave and silent and not to chatter. I wonder whether there is not a sort of instinctive feeling that unseen powers have been at work and that nothing must be done to provoke them further?

No doubt after the first outburst of wailing from the women of the kraal, there was great decorum at Xaliswa's home. I can imagine that she herself would steal away and sit down in the cool shade of her hut, while a messenger would be sent to the headman of the location, who, in his turn, would report the affair at the Government Office. One by one near relatives of the deceased woman would come to the kraal. They would greet one another with few words, realising that it was an occasion when silence means so much more than speech.

Some of the younger men would begin to dig a grave in the open veld, not more than one hundred yards from the kraal. They would know quite well that the body could not be removed from sight until the *eye* of the Government had been there, but, at least, they could prepare its last resting-place. After digging down some five feet, they would stop the downward excavation and would scope out the little chamber at the side into which, according to custom, the body is placed.

All this time poor Xaliswa sits alone and dumb in the shadow of her hut. She alone could tell the thoughts that passed within her mind at that time. Was there a dull feeling of satisfaction that at last the struggle was over and could never return ? Or was there an awful feeling of condemnation as though the light of the sun had been turned into blackness ? Or was there a fearful wonder about the consequences of her deed—an effort to recall all that she had heard about the penalty for murder under the English law ? Or was there a longing for sympathy—a great desire to call her child Nonjinji to her arms and to hold her there ? Or was there a keen, passionate craving that she herself could be a child again, and could hide her head on her mother's breast ?

*   *   *   *

Xaliswa waited in prison at Umtata, only twelve miles from her own home, until the judge should come to finish her trial. " When would he come ? " It did not seem to matter in the least to other people when he came—whether he came in a few months or in a few years—nor did it seem to matter in the least how much she suffered in the suspense of waiting. She was in a new world, where every one went on his or her own way without taking the least notice of her. She felt sometimes that people were looking at her and speaking of her as one who had murdered another, but it was in the far-off kind of way that people might look at a wild animal caught in a cage.

People might be interested in her as a criminal but not as a person. She herself was of no concern to anybody. She thought of her old mother, Mazihle, living beyond the Gungululu hill at Zandukwane. It seemed ages since she saw her. Had she, too, quite forgotten Xaliswa ? Was it a matter of indifference to her whether she lived or died ? And Nonjinji, who had never left her for a single day until that terrible day— had Nonjinji, too, quite forgotten ?

Then, one day, came a great surprise. It was on a Sunday—the day when white people shut up their stores and do no work. Even at home her own people used to say that it was unlucky to work on Sunday, and they were wont to lay aside their hoes and to seek some pleasant kraal where the Kafir corn had been well ground and the beer was " ripe." In prison it had not made much difference to her whether it was Sunday or a weekday, except that a native *mshumayeli* (preacher) had come, and the prisoners had all been gathered together to listen to his preaching and prayers and to sing hymns. Xaliswa had often heard of preachers before, and she had seen the big houses where the *amagqoboka* (Christians, literally, " pierced ones ") had met together. But she had never met a preacher herself, and she had always been told that they were men to be avoided, because they taught the people to break away from the customs of their fathers. She had known one or two people who became Christians, and she was told that these people had displeased the spirits of their ancestors, and that they would be punished by sickness or by barrenness or by the death of their children.

On this particular Sunday she went with the other prisoners to the service, but she had understood very little. She liked the hymns, and was always sorry when they were finished. They seemed to speak to her

of her mother and Nonjinji. When the service was
over, she had gone back to her cell, and then, to her
surprise, the preacher came to talk to her. Perhaps
he was going to reproach her for her crime. Even
amongst "red" people murder was accounted as a
very bad thing, but she knew that Christians went
further, and said beer-drinks and many other things
to which she had been accustomed were bad.

But the preacher did not talk about her sin. He
talked about One who cared for her, and as he spoke
it seemed to her that he, too, cared. She had thought
that no one cared, and these words were like the
first rain of the spring coming down upon the sun-
baked earth and trickling down the parched brown
blades of grass to the thirsty roots. For a long time
her heart had seemed to be dead, and she had never
cried, but now, to her own surprise, she felt the warm
tears dropping on her hands. She did not understand
very much that first day, but she longed for Sunday
to come again, because the preacher said he would
talk again with her on the following Sunday. He came
again and again, and the scales dropped from her eyes.
She saw as she had never seen the horror of her sin,
but she saw also something far greater than her sin—
the amazing love and mercy of God.

*   *   *   *

The judge came and went away again. Xaliswa
was guilty and condemned to die. The preacher
had told her that she must not be afraid to die, because
Jesus Christ, the Son of God, had died, and by His
death had conquered death, and by His rising again
had opened to us the gate of everlasting life. But it
seemed strange that she should die now she knew so
much. If she had known before what she knew now
she could never have committed that terrible crime.
She was taught now that the Lord of all was reviled,

and He reviled not again, that He was brought as a
sheep before the shearers and was dumb, that He was
mocked and spitted upon, and scourged, and cruelly
put to death. And He tells His people to love their
enemies, and to pray for those who do them wrong.
She had not known this. If she had known it, she
would have found it very difficult, and perhaps she
would have failed, but at least she could never have
lifted the axe against another.

It seemed strange, too, that she should die without
being able to tell her mother and Nonjinji all that she
knew. No one could tell them in the same way that
she could how the light had come into her soul. The
preacher told her she must pray to God—the Father
who loves all—for her mother and for Nonjinji. He
said that prayer is like a key which God puts into our
hands, and that with it we are able to unlock many
a fast-closed door. He told her that God's ways are
not our ways, and that we must believe that all things
will work together for good to them who love Him.

*   *   *   *

The preacher was quite right. God's ways are
not our ways. Xaliswa did not pay the extreme
penalty of death, and her life was no doubt spared
to her for God's own good purpose. Twenty years
was a long time to spend away from her own country,
and away from her mother and Nonjinji. The preacher
told her that she could find God in prison as well as
in her home on the veld, and he was right. Xaliswa
had been baptised now, and had become a child of
God, and a member of the Body of Jesus Christ. The
Bishop, too, had come to lay his hands on her that she
might receive the gift of the Holy Ghost.

A few weeks ago I received the following letter
from Xaliswa:—". . . I got your letter . . . I was
so glad of my child's photo. It made me quite happy.

I can't repay you for your kindness, but God will repay it all. I am so well, and I pray night and day to God to get home again and see you all well again. My work is not hard that I am doing. I will also be glad if you also pray for me in the day or night or any time and ask God, and I will do the same just to get home one day. I got no more news, but hope to hear a lot from home. I could never think our Heavenly Father was such a good Man, but to-day I can see what He does for sinners. So I hope to be a better woman. . . . I must let you know I can read and am getting on quite well. I knew nothing about God, but I know where to find Him now, and also show others the right way. I will be glad if my family try and find God like I have. My heart is not sore that I am here, because I found my Lord here and will keep in the right way. If I am outside I would never have found my Lord like I got Him now. . . . I can see and also feel that I am a child of God now, and hope to remain one till my dying day."

Quite clearly our friend is beginning to cast her care upon One who cares for her, and she does not sign her name *Xaliswa* (burdened with care), but *Sarah Jane Makubone.*

P.S. May, 1924.—The above was written more than twelve years ago, and much has happened since in the life of our friend. She is no longer living behind the high walls of the House of Correction at Cape Town. She is free, and, of her own choice, she is in part charge of the hostel for girls who come to the Mission to learn weaving. She also helps in the teaching of spinning at the Weaving School. There was a complete reconciliation with her husband's relations, and the old name *Xaliswa* (burdened with care) is for us dead and buried with all its implications

CHAPTER X

JESSIE'S HOME (*KULO-JESSIE*)

"He was learning one of the great truths of life, a truth
that so many fail to learn—that it is not in isolation but as
a member of a body that a man finds his fullest self-expression."

"A human life, I think, should be well-rooted in some spot
of a native land where it may get the love of tender kinship
for the face of the earth . . . for the sounds and accents that
haunt it. . . ."—DANIEL DERONDA.

"**C**AN you tell me which is Skenjana's kraal?"
I asked of two young Native men when I
reached Mjika. "There are many kraals of
the Skenjana family. Which one does the Mfundisi
want?" "I want the one where there is a girl who
is very ill," I said. "Oh! you mean *kulo-Jessie*"—
Jessie's home. The word for home is not expressed,
but it is quite understood. That missing word stands
for something very precious. In the case of Jessie
Skenjana it stands for three or four huts on the veld.
They are good, well-built huts, and they are kept in
good repair. Close to the hut is the cattle kraal,
not just the usual enclosure of *amahlahla* (branches),
but hedged round with live aloes, and below this there
is a garden of peach trees. Beyond the garden is the
veld, and beyond the veld the mountains.

But is this all that the missing word stands for?
Does it only stand for huts and kraal and garden and

veld ? Of course not. None of us are such material-
ists as to think so. Two men stood together once on
the top of the great Matoppo Hills, looking with the
fullest enjoyment at the wonderful stretch of country
before them. One of the two said to the other, " I
want to see these valleys filled with homes, homes,
homes ! " Neither the speaker, Cecil Rhodes, nor his
companion, Earl Grey, were thinking of a collection of
houses. They were thinking of the best form of human
fellowship.

The word " home " gathers up all that is most
precious in human life. It speaks to us of the " golden
age "—that age which is golden whether it belongs
to a dark-skinned child of the veld, or to the fair-
skinned child of an English home. It speaks to Jessie,
as it speaks to you and to me, of the wonderful love of
the one who in *isi-Xosa* child-language, as well as in
English, is called " Mama " (the word is the same,
but the accentuation is different). It speaks of one
whom brown child-lips call " Tata," and white child-
lips call " Daddy." It speaks of " Bude " (brother)
and " Sissie " (sister). It speaks of years when all is
shared, and no one said ought was his own, not even
that little doll made of a mealie cob. No wonder,
when she was so ill, that Jessie felt the call of home.
But I am anticipating. I will return to the call later.

I always associate Jessie with Selina Sitole who is
now at rest. Selina had been ill with lung trouble
long before she came to St. Lucy's Hospital. " God's
writing " was quite clear, writ large upon her face, even
in those days. She was plainly given to us not to
heal, but to tend and to care for, and to give back to
God. In spite of her natural cheerfulness and hope-
fulness she herself did not really think otherwise. It
was when Selina was so ill that I first got to know Jessie.
Possibly I had seen her before as a schoolgirl at Mjika.

but it was only some time after she left school, when
she came as a probationer to St. Lucy's Hospital, that
I really came to know her.

We have been wonderfully fortunate in our Native
probationers. One cannot doubt that the day will
come when Native girls will bear the full responsibility
of trained nurses. Indeed, there are already a few
fully qualified Native nurses. At St. Lucy's we are
not entitled to train nurses, but excellent work has
been done in training probationers. Jessie took
kindly to the work from the very first. Quiet and self-
possessed in manner, strong and capable in body and
mind, she seemed quite the right person. Here was
a girl, one felt, who ought not to be content with being
a probationer. She appeared to have a real vocation
for nursing and ought to go on to get her full training.

One day, some time after Selina had died, when I
went to the Hospital I found Jessie, to my great surprise, not nursing others but herself a patient. She
was in a bed on the stoep, but she looked so well that
it was difficult to believe that she was ill. I took it
for granted that it·was some trifling ailment and did
not even ask what was the matter. Constantly I
expected to see her about again, and it came as a great
surprise to hear the Sister speaking a little anxiously
about her. I began to see how ill she was when she
came to her Communion in the Hospital Chapel. All
the spring had gone out of her movements, and the
cough told its own tale. And yet how difficult it was
to believe that the disease had taken any real hold of
her. The face looked still so young and full and
unmarked by suffering. She never complained, and
always had a bright welcome for her visitors.

One day, when she was getting weaker, I could see
that she had something to say to me which was a little
difficult to be said. Her mother, it seems, had been

to see her, and had been suggesting that she should be taken home. It was quite natural both that her mother should wish to have her child, and that Jessie should wish to be at home. But evidently it was not quite easy for Jessie to decide. St. Lucy's had come to mean a good deal to her, so much so that it was difficult to think of saying good-bye to it. At last, however, the decision was made, and a waggon came to take Jessie to Mjika.

A week or two later I got a little note from Jessie. Evidently she was suffering a good deal, and she said, " In my prayer I say these words, ' Lord, give me rest from my sufferings in any way that Thou seest. I will accept the way that Thou givest.' "

The next note was written by some one else at her dictation, and she spoke of Father Chard coming to communicate her. Then it was that I had a chance of going to see her. I had never been to her kraal before, and was not quite sure as to its whereabouts, but " kulo-Jessie " seemed to be fairly well known.

Such a bright look of welcome greeted me as Jessie's mother took me into her hut. Poor girl! she had evidently lost ground a good deal since she left St. Lucy's. Her face looked worn and suffering, and it was with difficulty that she could lift herself at all. I was glad to find that her hut was large and cool, and the head of the bed was brought right up to the open doorway, so that she was almost out of doors. I was glad, too, that her eyes would always be greeted by so fair a prospect. It was a good spot for a human life to be " well-rooted," and to find the " tender kinship for the face of the earth . . . for the sounds and accents that haunt it."

As I looked out from Jessie's doorway I felt that it was essentially a neighbourly country. On the veld we do not ask, " Who is my neighbour ? " On all the ridges, which cross and re-cross one another, like waves driven by opposing winds, are the kraals of the people, and everywhere, from every kraal you trace the little paths worn by brown feet in the service of neighbourliness. True, they go to the shop, to the church, to the school, to the spring, to the forest; but they also go from one home to another. You feel that these are not ornamental paths, nor are they paths laid out for passers-by, like the priest and the Levite of the parable. They are paths of neighbourliness, and in them I seemed to see a parable of κοινωνία —fellowship—brotherhood. There is on the veld an absence of snobbishness. There is no sign of exclusiveness, no eager rivalry of ostentation. Jessie was amongst neighbours.

And beyond the furthest ridges of the mountains which "stand about" the kraals to be a perpetual reminder that "even so standeth the Lord round about His people," and in the deep ravines of those mountains where the forests lose themselves in hidden depths, there is "a cloud and smoke by day and the shining of a flaming fire by night." And in the rock-buttresses of those mountains there is to be found many "a tabernacle for a shadow in the daytime from the heat, and for a place of refuge, and for a covert from storm and from rain." As I looked at those mountains from the doorway of Jessie's hut I felt they had many words to say to those who had ears to hear. Here were the "accents that haunt" Jessie's home.

No! I was not surprised that Jessie should have felt the call of home. But she had not forgotten the other home—the Hospital at St. Cuthbert's—and she was eager to hear all I could tell her of her friends there. There was no word of regret, no grudging of the offering she had made when she went there to be a probationer. What an offering it was! There had been such a

short ministry, and then months of pain and weariness
with scarcely any relief.

A week or two later Jessie's aunt came up one
Sunday morning to bring Jessie's own word that she
was leaving us, and that she wanted the *umsimelelo*,
the staff of support, and the *umpako*, the food for the
journey. When I reached kulo-Jessie that morning,
carrying with me the Blessed Sacrament, she just
whispered to me, " I want to go, and I want the food
of the journey."

After her Communion and some prayers, I asked
for a hymn-book. At a sign from Jessie her mother
went to her box. A very precious thing is that box,
in which a few treasures are kept. She found a hymn-
book, but Jessie was not satisfied, and whispered, " It
must be the new one." The new one was found and
given to me. I could not help noticing how carefully
and neatly it had been covered with some grey material,
and in a little pocket were all Jessie's Sunday School
cards. I asked for her favourite hymn, and she
answered without hesitation, " Nkosi ndikumbule."
This is a translation of " Lord Jesus, think on me."
There are times when one feels that the choice of a
hymn is an inspiration. This was one of those times.
I sang it all to her softly. Then she stopped me and
called her mother. I heard the whispered injunction
to her mother to make me a cup of tea. Here was
the innate courtesy—the instinct of generous
hospitality asserting itself even at the moment of
extreme suffering. Then at her wish I sang, " The
King of Love my Shepherd is."

> " In death's dark vale I fear no ill
> With Thee, dear Lord, beside me ;
> Thy rod and staff my comfort still,
> Thy cross before to guide me."

I knew as I said " Good-bye " to Jessie that the Peace

of God which passeth all understanding had indeed flowed into her soul as the rising tide of a quiet sea steals gently up the shore, and flows into the deep pool. The call to the true home had come. I expect there was still to be a little waiting time, and then the doors of that wider world would be opened, and Jessie would find a welcome so far beyond the reach of our conception and yet most really the welcome of Home.

I felt thankful that the real " kulo-Jessie " was neither at St. Lucy's or Mjika. It is in that real home that Jessie will find the meaning of both. There she will re-find the paths of neighbourliness of Mjika— the true fellowship—and there she will also re-find the ministry of St. Lucy's, for there " His servants shall serve Him."

CHAPTER XI

A GLIMPSE FROM AN OPEN WINDOW AT ST. LUCY'S HOSPITAL

" These hearts were woven human joys and cares."

THERE is nothing quite like the silence of the early dawn on the veld.

The window is open, and the eye travels over the Mission glebe, beyond the Ncolosi stream, which borders it, to the soft, green slopes on the other side, up to the top of the ridges where the kraals are plentiful—even the huts of the people seem to be under a covenant of silence—away to further ridges, and yet further, until it rests on the forest-clad hills across the valley of the Inxu River. The eye sees this and more. The ear expects to hear sounds and finds *silence.*

It is silence vibrant with speech. It is silence full of the Word, by Whom all things were made. " His the primal language, His the eternal silences." In that silence the soul learns silence, " My soul is silent unto God." It is the silence of a great mystery, like the silence of worship and adoration after the prayer of Consecration.

The first sound to break in upon the silence brings us down from the Mount of Transfiguration into the valley of pain. It comes from Regina, who sleeps on the stoep outside and greets the early morning light

with a fit of coughing. Poor Regina ! It is not many
years ago that she and her husband built a new home
on the shoulder of Bele Mountain overlooking the
Mission. Jonathan, her husband, is an active man
who has lived all his life on the Mission. He was
trained in stone-cutting by our old friend George
Home, who so bravely came out from Scotland with
lungs far gone, and began to build our church at
St. Cuthbert's and the Cathedral at Umtata. When
Jonathan built his new kraal on the hill he quarried
from the hill-side some good stone posts, and fenced
in a nice piece of ground for a garden. As a mason he
is always in demand, and he commands good wages.
No doubt he has been investing his savings in a few
cattle and sheep and goats, so the home is
comfortable.

" We were so pleased with our new home," said
Regina to me one day, " but I have never been well
since we went there." I asked if her children came to
see her in the hospital when they came out of school,
and she said, " They came at first, but I saw that they
went away with sore hearts, so I told them not to come."
Regina's condition is serious, and her cough racks her
a good deal.

The sun has now risen on the world outside, and
the hospital, which has been left at night to the night-
nurse and the patients, begins to stir with sounds of a
general awakening. Patience comes to my ward to
sweep and clean. Patience is one of the native
probationers, and she looks quite business-like in the
white cap and apron and blue print dress. She is
a diminutive little person, demure and serious for her
years. She came to the Mission as a boarder from a
kraal on the Bele, and most of her relations were
heathen, but the work of conversion had begun.
It is difficult to realise that Patience was ever

anything else than she is now. I can only think of
her as a staid, serious little person who wanted
knowing. I cannot think of her in a red blanket
running wild amongst the heathen. I have to ask
myself if I can ever remember Patience as naughty.
I have no doubt that the Sisters would smile at this
and tell me that Patience has given them some very
bad half-hours. But now she is a communicant, a
teacher in the Sunday School, and a probationer in
the hospital.

I am aroused from my reverie by a small voice
speaking in Xosa, "Father, you have not drunk your
milk in the night. Sister says you will never get
strong unless you drink your milk."

"Oh, Patience, they treat me very badly here.
They are always stuffing me with food."

"No, Father, they don't treat you badly : they
want you to get well. Look at Gladys : she was very
ill, but she is going home to-day. Sister says she got
well because she ate her food."

"Patience, you are always scolding me. Go up
to the Mission House and ask for my boots. I want to
go out to-day."

"Shall I ask the doctor if I may fetch your boots ? "

I relapse, and Patience knows that she has won
the victory.

There begins to be a good deal of movement outside,
and as I look out of the window I see out-patients
beginning to arrive. What a delightful waiting-room
they have got ! There is no solemn butler in livery
to usher them in. There are no lounge chairs or sofas.
There is no need to provide illustrated paper and
Punch. The waiting-room is very extensive. It is
the open veld.

On the form of application for a grant towards a
new school there is one question which amuses us

out here. " What is the extent of the playground attached to the school ? " The playground is, of course, the veld—this veld, which sweeps past all limitations to the furthest distances and beyond. That, too, is the waiting-room.

Patients don't come on a wet day. So it is not often that shelter is needed, other than that of the trees, which give shade from the hot sun. And seats are not provided because Mother Earth is kind, and because, out here, we do not take kindly to the custom of " stopping halfway " when we sit down.

I said there was no liveried official to welcome the patients, but I was wrong. Bransby, the orderly, is always there in his nice white jacket, and it is to him that the patients first go on their arrival, so that he may write down upon forms their names and other particulars. He sits at a little table on the stoep, and quite lends dignity to the proceedings. Bransby's father, who died many years ago, was one of the earliest Christians on the Mission, and he was with Bishop Key in the first years of his work amongst the Pondomisi. Bransby has been at St. Lucy's for several years, and is quite a useful person. He also sings in the choir, and assists sometimes as thurifer.

There is no waiting for introductions amongst the patients as they arrive. They come from east, west, north, and south. There are Fingoes, and Hlubis, and Pondos, and Xosas. Many of them have never seen one another before, but out here we belong to a big family, and tongues soon begin to wag with astonishing freedom.

Out here sick folk—native sick folk—do not mind noise. We don't put straw down outside, nor do we restrain the tongues of the out-patients. Except for that one critical moment when they exhibit that unruly member to the doctor, they seem to give it no rest.

As I lie in my ward and watch them, I begin to think that some at least have begun to be healed of their diseases before they reach the doctor—healed by overflowing good fellowship.

One morning I persuaded myself that the noise was too great, so I asked Patience to tell some of the offenders that there were sick folk inside, and they must talk quietly. At once I began to regret the message. I felt sure they must know that it was a cantankerous white man who sent such a message ; no native would have thought of it. Just for a few minutes there was quiet whispering, and then, almost to my relief, out burst the voices again.

"Good morning, Grandmother," said a middle-aged man to a woman not much older than himself—it was a relationship of courtesy, not of blood or affinity—"are you well, Grandmother ? "

"Yes, child of my father, I am well, but I am not well on account of my daughter here."

"And what is the matter with your daughter, Grandmother ? " Then follows the usual graphic description. There is no hesitation, no labouring for words, no sort of reserve, out here we know all about our insides, and we are not ashamed to speak of them.

While the talking goes on, a rough, wooden sleigh, drawn by four oxen, halts outside the gate of the hospital. A bundle, wrapped round in a red blanket, is lying on the sacks, half filled with grass, which cover the bottom of the sleigh. After some consultation, Bransby, the orderly, produces a stretcher, and the bundle is laid thereon and carried into the hospital. This is a new in-patient. Her husband, a "red" Native, had come a few days earlier to tell the doctor about his wife. "She had a fall," he said, "and hurt herself." This was a very euphemistic way of putting the matter, as, in course of cross-examination, the doctor discovered, as he had suspected, that the fall had been induced by what the husband discreetly called a " push." So here the poor woman had been brought, to find her only chance of life in an operation.

If you come to think of it, it shows an amazing degree of confidence for these heathen folk, full of superstition, and hopelessly ignorant, to bring such a case here to the hospital. At one time it would have been useless to suggest it, but nowadays the hospital is known, and the doctor is known. Many a heathen man who has been brought into the hospital by the hands of others has gone home healed in body and somewhat enlightened in mind. Sometimes he has gone back enlightened and healed in soul too.

> " Oh, in what divers pains they met !
> Oh, with what joy they went away ! "

By this time it is 8.30 a.m., and the doctor has come down from the Mission House. Sometimes he has already begun the day at 6.30 with operations. I now hear the tinkle of a little bell, the gathering together of the people, and then complete silence. I just catch the number of a hymn, and then comes one of the old familiar tunes, led by a few strong and true voices. I cannot catch the Xosa words of the hymn unless it is very familiar. And then, in a clear voice which carries every word to me in my ward, the doctor reads a passage from the Gospel narrative, and then he prays.

Some there are who, I am quite sure, value this greatly, Regina for one, and also that nice Presbyterian preacher, Joseph, who is lying in the men's ward. I hope there are some amongst the out-patients also who value it. It may seem strange to the heathen, but I cannot help feeling that it may arouse questions in them which some day may find the right answer

and may stir in them past influences for good that
have been lying dormant.

Again the bell tinkles, and out-patients begin to be
admitted by turn to their interview with the doctor.

Dinner-time comes, and although the crowd may
have melted away there may still be a few people to
be seen. The doctor runs away for a brief half-hour,
comes back to see these few remaining out-patients,
and then I hear the sound of his car as he hurries off to
visit one or two cases which cannot be brought to him.

Perhaps during the morning two or three new
patients have been admitted to the hospital. How
unutterably strange it must seem to some of them!
Just think of that "red" woman who was brought in
this morning from a heathen kraal. She has never
before been inside a European house except the trader's
store. She comes into this strange building, with
its doors and windows and tables and chairs. She
lies for the first time in her life upon something raised
from the ground. The red blankets—the inseparable
companions of a lifetime—are removed. She feels
the unfamiliar touch of the white sheet, her head
rests back for the first time on a soft pillow. She
looks round at the pictures on the walls, the crucifix,
the many unfamiliar objects. Perhaps for a moment
she feels the most lonely woman in the world. And
then, little by little the strangeness wears away.
Little by little the kindness and care and love of the
Sister and nurses who minister to her speak to her heart.
She begins to talk to the patient who lies nearest to
her, and she asks questions. At last, one day, she
knows that she is amongst friends, and she finds that
the hospital is a "home." And perhaps she learns a
greater lesson still—that those who nurse her are
ministering to One who said, "I was sick, and ye
visited Me."

*   *   *   *

I omitted the very foreground of the picture—
Sammie, the favoured cat, lying in cushioned state
on a chair just outside my window, watching the
proceedings with a sleepy indifference born of long
familiarity and over-careful feeding.   My apologies to
Sammie for reserving him for a postscript !

CHAPTER XII

THE NEWS FROM NCEMBU

"He [the Native] has a natural responsiveness to the notion of goodness and all that is connected with it in religion."

*E*ZASE-NCEMBU. There is a word to be filled in here. It is a word so dear to the heart of a Native that he instinctively supplies it. It is a plural noun that is missing. So far as the grammatical construction is concerned it might be almost anything—cattle, sheep, or just things. But every one knows that it is *indaba* (news). The news from Ncembu. *Indaba* is a word very precious to the Native. Perhaps there is only one word equally precious, and that is *ikaya* (home). Both words speak of social needs. A man without a home is an impossible person—he is not a man at all. If it were possible for a man to be homeless it would be a disgrace to the society to which he belonged. A word has had to be coined (*itshipa*) to describe such a man, and even then it refers not exactly to a man without a home, but to the man who deserts his true home, and vanishes into the hidden places of the white man's cities.

If a person without a home barely deserves the name "man," what shall we say of a man who has no *indaba* ? He must be a man who is secretive, who loves darkness rather than light, the sort of man who would eat his food alone and smoke his pipe alone. He is the kind

84

THE CHURCH OF THE ASCENSION, NCEMBU,

facing p. 84.

A NATIVE CHIEF'S KRAAL.

PREPARATIONS FOR AN OPENING MEETING.

facing p. 85.

of man who does not open his pouch to a friend, and is guilty of the unpardonable sin of grudging. Such a man must be shunned. By his very acts he proclaims himself to be an *igqwira* (sorcerer). *Ikaya* and *indaba* make up the inalienable possessions of manhood.

Ezase-Ncembu means, then, "the news from Ncembu," and Ncembu is the name of a bright and merry little stream which flows through the country of the ama-Tola and gives its name to the locality. I imagine that a certain blue lily must grow in the neighbourhood of that stream, as *i-Ncembu* is the name of the edible bulb of that lily.

From our point of view Ncembu is a daughter of St. Cuthbert's, a big daughter who has married and has a kraal (*umzi*) of her own, and two or three children. The news to-day from Ncembu requires a headline and large capital letters, something like this :

CHURCH OF THE ASCENSION, NCEMBU— DEDICATION.

In England as you sit in one of your noble churches you may well be puzzled to think how such a building ever came to be evolved. You may even go and ransack your library to search out the various stages of its evolution. Here, on the veld, history is written before your eyes. Within a few miles of Ncembu you may see a cave which only a few years ago was the dwelling-place of the "Bushmen"—those diminutive, yellow-skinned, wizened little folk who represent a very primitive type of man. Like the fowls of the air, they neither sowed nor reaped nor did they gather into barns. Very unlike the lilies of the field in most things they were like them in this, that they neither toiled nor did they spin. Their raiment was chiefly provided for them when they came into the world. These Bushmen lived by killing, and very cunning they became in hunting their prey.

Then we see the next stage, where the simplest of huts—made of wattle and grass—replace the cave, and animals, instead of being killed, have been caught and tamed and milked and inspanned. The hut is further developed, until at last it is replaced by a building of more serious dimensions, such as the old church at Ncembu, from which we have now emerged to take possession of this large stone building.

A stranger coming upon this church would, I think, say, "Well, here are people who did not do what it is taken for granted in the Bible every one who is not a fool will do—they did not, when they planned their church, sit down and reckon out the cost of completing it. They began well with solid, well-built stone walls, but evidently they began too well and could not carry out the original design. The roof does not worthily crown the labours of those who built the walls."

If the stranger is a man well versed in building he will at once think to himself how differently the church would have looked if, instead of this great expanse of iron innocent of any ceiling—naked and unashamed —we had built pillars to support a clerestory with a central lofty roof. Let us at once plead guilty. Our defence is that we began to build before the Great War, and just when we wanted to bring the church to completion we were faced with terribly inflated prices and an impossible task. Nobly friends came forward to help us in our difficulty, but even with such help we could not aspire to architectural delights. Some day it may be possible for our successors to carry out a more worthy design for the roof. In the meantime we refuse to be over-critical, and we rejoice and give thanks for a church glorious in its possibilities. After all, it is a great achievement and, even as it is,

it makes a great appeal. As it stands there on its
lofty eminence looking out over wide stretches of veld
away to the blue peaks of the Drakensberg it seems
to say, "Come, my children, and learn that the
Heart of God is large and wide and all-embracing.
Here within these stone walls is the kraal (the fold)
of God, in which you will find shelter and protection
and warmth and love.".

The church can claim, at least, that in one respect
it is unique. Every single stone has been squared
and laid by one pair of hands, and it took that man
twelve years to complete his job. You must not think
that this excellent man scrupulously worked his eight
hours a day throughout all the days of the year except
Sundays and Bank Holidays ! That is not our way
on the veld. Work, we say, was made for man, and
not man for work. We like to have time to salute our
friends, to exchange news, to smoke a friendly pipe
with the passer-by. Nor are we monopolists of a
trade out here. A man may be a builder, but he is
also a tiller of the soil, and a small farmer, and on
occasions a lawyer and many other things. We say
that Jonathan Zondani spent some twelve years of
his life upon the building of this church, but you must
make allowance for other pursuits as well, not to speak
of the fact that during that time he lost one wife and
married another. You must also remember that,
when the people at Ncembu got tired of feeding their
builder, Jonathan would lay aside his tools and walk
home (some thirty miles), until he was persuaded to
try again. Nevertheless, make as many deductions
as you like, I am still inclined to think that Jonathan
deserves to be knighted and to have a bronze statue
erected to his honour ! Sir Jonathan Zondani would
sound rather well !

You must not think that Jonathan was wholly

unaided. Ask the good Native Priest, Jemuel Pamla, about that. He will tell you that he himself spent many a weary hour working with his own hands in quarrying stone, and many still more weary hours persuading, coaxing, cajoling, pressing, urging, driving the people of the location to do their share of the quarrying and carting, etc. He will also tell you that he himself is poorer to the extent of a silver watch owing to the quarrying. Having divested himself one day of coat and waistcoat, he applied himself with vigour to his task. To his horror, when he next looked up, he espied the end of his waistcoat protruding from the mouth of a cow, which was chewing the bulk of it with great contentment. Unfortunately, in that same waistcoat pocket was a silver watch, bought at the price of careful savings, and this was in that part of the waistcoat which had already been chewed and swallowed ! Nor must we forget the work that has been done in the carpenter's shop at St. Cuthbert's and elsewhere, nor all the planning which fell on the Father Superior.

So to-day, as we stand within the walls of the completed church, we give thanks to God for all who have helped to build this church to His glory. But there are two persons whom we particularly single out for our gratitude. One of these two is beyond the veil, the other is with us still. One is an Englishman who never set foot in this country. The other is a Native who only at the close of a long life became a Christian.

The one is George Dearden of beloved memory who has left to us a rich legacy of saintliness as well as many material gifts, given always with the utmost hiddenness and humility. He it was who primarily enabled us to roof our church. I saw him when I was last in England a few years ago, and, as usual, he wanted to hear all about the work, and he pressed me to tell

him of our needs. On the following day I received
a letter from him enclosing a cheque for £200 to be
given anonymously towards the roof of Ncembu Church.
In his letter he said that if I succeeded in getting
another £100 towards the £400 required he would give
the remaining £100. That is the kind of letter which
sends you down on your knees. Generous friends
came forward with gifts, and I was able to claim the
fulfilment of that promise.

The other person whom we remember to-day is
Bikwe, the aged chief, who forty-one years ago, when
he was about fifty, led his clan of the ama-Tola out
of Pondoland to settle with them at Ncembu. He it
was who opened the door to missionary work amongst
his people, and throughout all these years has been a
staunch and true friend to St. Cuthbert's. In his
old age, to our great joy, he became a Christian,
and very touching it is to see him brought here by
willing hands to receive his Communion in the church
which he had been so largely instrumental in giving
to God.

The church may have its architectural defects,
but it certainly looked very beautiful in our eyes when
the doors were thrown open and we escorted the
Bishop, through the ranks of a large congregation,
to take his place in the sanctuary. The Bishop, who
sang the Mass, also preached to the people and begged
them to remember what this beautiful church was
to mean to them and their children.

With great joy and with real spirit the people
sang their Eucharist, and afterwards, at the opening
meeting, they showed their gratitude by the readiness
of their response. In cash alone about £40 was
contributed.

Ziyapela apa ezase-Ncembu—which, being interpreted in the vulgar tongue, means, " Here ends the

news from Ncembu." But even as I write the words
I know that this is not the end, but only the very
beginning of a work which by the grace of God will be
carried on under the guidance and leadership of Jemuel
Pamla, a humble servant (δοῦλος) of Jesus Christ.

P.S.—When the MS. of this book was out of my
hands our faithful friend Jemuel Pamla was called to
rest.

The illness which finally took him away from us
was disease in the upper part of the spine, and for some
eight months he was quite helpless and seldom free
from pain. Throughout all these months he was
wonderfully patient. He was too ill to read himself
or even to attend for long to any one else reading,
but he liked to hear of the work and of his out-stations.
When I was about to set out on a round of visits to his
stations he used to say to me, " Father, tell the people
that they are in my heart and in my prayers—especially
the preachers."

The last time I saw him alive he was evidently in
pain and found difficulty in speaking, but he made a
great effort and said, with great distinctness, " *Father,
ndifuna ukuba icebo lika-Tixo lenziwe* " (" I want the
will of God to be done "). Those were the last words
he spoke to me. He died early the next morning and
his body was laid to rest in our cemetery next to that
of Bishop Alan Gibson.

A friend of ours who was once Magistrate of Tsolo
district, when he heard of Jemuel's death, wrote that
" he was one of the most simple and genuine souls that
I have known, white or black." Another friend, a
School Inspector whose work was once in this district,
wrote, " Though I knew him so slightly I feel a sense
of personal loss. I shall never forget the few days I
had the privilege of spending with him at Ncembu

and Gqaqala.   He pointed to what a Native ministry
might be.   I shall always feel glad I knew him."
   I could tell of many touching expressions of love
and grief, but I have written enough to show that in
spite of his shy reserve Jemuel was greatly loved and
respected by men who differed greatly in their outlook
on life.   I cannot wish or pray for anything better for
the Church among the Natives of these parts than that
God will raise up from amongst them more Priests
after the likeness of Jemuel Pamla.

CHAPTER XIII

JEMUEL PAMLA'S SERMON IN LENT

" The Friar always regarded the Church as the Sponsa Christi and His other self, whose duty it was to bear with sinners in order to save them eventually."

IT is, I believe, understood in some parts, that a sermon at Sung Mass should not exceed ten minutes. Personally I am inclined to approve of that understanding, especially when I am either the preacher or the celebrant. This morning, however, although I was the celebrant, I listened not merely with patience, but with great satisfaction to a sermon of about an hour. I did not regret one single word. The church was a round hut, with a black soot-festooned roof. There was no window, and the doorway was exceedingly narrow and low.

Outside was a burning sun : inside were some thirty people, all of whom were, presumably, at least as hot as I was. Flies swarmed about us, settling upon hot faces and hands. As I sat on a small stool listening to the preacher, I could look out of the narrow doorway upon the hottest of hot valleys, down which the Tsitsa River slowly wanders, walled in by high hills. The sun beat down with pitiless force upon a land already exhausted by drought and heat.

Only a few weeks ago that valley was laughing and singing with a promise of plenty—a promise unknown

for years.   At last it had seemed that the heavy cloud
of difficulty and famine was lifting, and in spite of the
scarcity of food, the hearts of the people were lightened,
and Hope raised up her head.   But burning suns and
parching winds had changed everything, and the hearts
of the people were heavy.

As I looked upon the congregation, it seemed to
me that the faces of the elder people were tired and
heavy.   At all times it is a congregation of struggling
and poor people, but now endurance had almost reached
its limit, and two or three families had already left their
kraals in the valley which they loved, to go as squatters
on the farms of Europeans, where at least they would
get food in return for their work.

I had asked the Native priest, Jemuel Pamla, to
preach, and as he stood there I wondered what he would
preach about.   It is Monday before Ash Wednesday,
and the obvious thing would be to speak of the call of
Mother Church to a new effort of penitence in Lent.
But was it possible to speak about Lent and fasting
to a people in such extremity ?   I felt that I should
have only one word to say, " My children, we read
that our Lord Jesus Christ was driven into the hard
and cruel wilderness to be tempted of the devil, and
it seems that you, who are the children of God, are
being called to follow Him.   This must be your Lent,
and may God, who loves you and calls you to victory,
bless and strengthen you in that trial."

I was thankful that I was not called upon to preach.
I knew quite well that my friend Jemuel would speak
from a heart warmed by prayer, and I knew, too,
that he would mean every word he spoke.   It is only
as I think of the sermon and as I attempt to write it
down upon paper, that I realise how impossible it is
to catch the genius of one language and to express it
in another.   Xosa lends itself wonderfully to living

speech. Like a tree in early spring it is bursting with life. It catches up the sighing of the winds, the music of the sunbeams, the joyous songs of the birds, the plaintive cries of the goats, the lowing of the cattle. It is charged with notes of human fellowship, with the low-toned chant of the milkers as they milk the cows, with the voices of the reapers as they bring back golden heads of maize from the lands, with the joyful clapping of hands at the marriage dance.

But Xosa does not lend itself so easily to pen and paper. Like a young colt with its head in a halter it seems to rebel against the loss of freedom. Still less does it lend itself to translation. But at least I must try to give some idea of a sermon which gripped me throughout, and left me wondering if I should ever try to preach again.

It was not that it was eloquent. It was that it was intensely real, vitally alive, and withal very homely. As usual, Jemuel began with a little word of introduction—perhaps some notice. I never knew any one give out notices in such an original way. I seldom succeed in repressing a smile, but I always realise that it was the one way, *par excellence*, to get a notice home to the minds of the people. He always speaks in a simple, unaffected way, but I am conscious of a real sense of fatherly authority behind his words.

"We don't like," he said one day in church, "to sit down to our food without washing our hands. Even if they do not look very dirty, it is always good to wash them. Don't forget that after Evensong the Father will be in church for confessions. Don't think it is only you who need confession. We *Abafundisi* need it just as much as you do. Indeed, it is the man who milks the cows who has to be most careful to wash his hands."

To-day, too, he began in a very informal and

colloquial way. I do not remember how he drifted
from the introductory remarks to the sermon proper.
I do not think there was a text. He carried us to
the banks of the Jordan and to the Baptism of Jesus.
" There was no stain on that bright dish which needed
cleansing. He was as the sun shining in its brightness.
. . . He it was who was led on to that dark desert to
meet with trial and temptation. He did not find there
even a mat to sleep upon, nor even a blanket which He
could borrow. At least we are better off than that.

" Lent calls us to a common effort. It is like the
i-Joyini "—the call of the Labour Agent, who gathers
together a number of young men for a common enterprise, that is, to " join " for work on the mines.

I could not help smiling as I thought of a party of
young men, with their blankets over their shoulders,
trudging along to the nearest railway station to take
the train to Johannesburg. One of the party would
be cheering the hearts of his companions by the strains
of a mouth organ. And yet the illustration was apt,
as these young men were called to leave all the joys and
delights of home, together with ease and independence,
for the severe discipline of six or nine months on the
mines. As the preacher had been speaking of the
" common enterprise " throughout the Church, I could
not help wondering if it would be a great shock to him
to find some day that the observance of Lent was the
exception, and not the rule ! His next words reassured
me somewhat. " Perhaps," he said, " some of you
will be going off to find work in the villages or on the
farms of Europeans, and you will find just the usual
life—the life of work and of pleasure, with plenty of
eating and drinking. That is your chance to remember
that you are the children of the Church. You know
what it is that the Church calls us to. This is the time
when we are to be like the hen which is sitting on her

eggs. The resolutions we make to-day are like those
eggs. We don't want our eggs to be rotten. If we
are faithful we shall see living things emerge from those
eggs. We can all do something. This time of difficulty
and drought is just an opportunity. Was it not the
poor widow who gave more than all ? Anything we
give now will be like the widow's mite—it will cost
much. Even a child can give something. When a
child comes home from working on the lands on a hot
day, how nice it is to stop at the stream and to drink,
and drink ! Well, you can just make up your mind
to cross that stream, and leave the water to the crabs.
Grown-up people have many things they can give up.
When a vessel is rusty there is nothing for it but to
take ashes and to scour it. To look at it then no one
would think you were cleaning it, but they would see
afterwards. It is the same with fasting, it cleanses,
even though it seems harsh treatment at the time."

I began to wonder, as he spoke of giving up tobacco
and snuff, if there was to be anything left at all, and
then he singled out the dearest of all joys to the Native,
the inexhaustible joy of cheerful gossip. Here, too,
there was room for offering—material for a rich gift.
" And how good it would be to use the time so saved
in prayer ! No one can expect to make progress without private prayer. Yes, it is indeed good to meet
together in prayer in the services, but you will be
milking into a leaking vessel unless you are also
saying your private prayers.

" But don't forget the importance of hiddenness.
Once as I was coming here I saw something very good.
I saw the people coming out of the service, and instead
of gathering together for gossip, I saw them go off to
the rocks for private prayer. That was good, but there
was just one little danger about it. It was too public.
There was such a danger of seeking credit. Go to the

guinea fowl to learn the lesson of hiddenness. Have
you ever found the wild fowl's eggs? No; she is far
too clever in hiding them. We must hide these Lent
eggs of ours. And we must beware of excuses. This is
just the time when we shall all of us find so many
reasons why we cannot keep a good Lent. Don't you
think that poor widow had good reasons why she
could not give? When I read about her I think that
the one good thing is to *swela*—to be in want."

At last he began to speak of the particular message
with which I had charged him. It was the gift of
£30 towards a church to be built at this very place.

"Here at Lower Ncele, we are rather like fowls,
trying to find a place to lay the eggs. We have no
church." Then with great joy he went on to tell the
good news.

By this time the people, who, by the bye, were all
sitting on the floor, were looking up with eager attention to the preacher. I could see the quick play of
wonder, surprise, and joy on the upturned faces.
"And now what are we going to do to show our
gratitude? We can never succeed in expressing our
thanks, but even a dog can wag its tail. And remember
this gift is to be to us a Bible, a revelation of the love
of God, a word straight from Him."

CHAPTER XIV

MATTINS AT BELE

" PLEASE, Father, these are the hymns we should like at this service." The speaker was Jack, a boy in Standard V. who, on Sundays, acts as a sort of curate to the blind preacher, Bango. Jack handed me a slip of paper with the numbers of six hymns. The service was to be Mattins, so I concluded I was to choose three out of the six. Then blind Bango himself came forward, and, very politely but very firmly, instructed me in the customary order and ritual of the proceedings.

I was quite made to feel that I was the " select preacher " who might possibly be asked to assist in other ways in addition to preaching, but who must conform to the regular " use."

" The vestry," said Bango, quite seriously, " is outside," and he turned his head to the open doorway with its outlook upon wild, rolling waves of veld. " And, Father, we begin with a hymn, and then we say the whole of the ' Dearly Beloved.' We do not leave any of it out." All this was said in Xosa, and it was spoken, I felt, with a slight emphasis, as much as to say, " I know your ways at St. Cuthbert's, how ready you are to clip and to cut, but here at the Bele we are not so concerned to save the minutes." " And then, Father, at the end, after we have taken off our

surplices in the *vestry*, we come back into the church
before the people go out."

The "church" to which Bango referred, and in
which our conversation took place, is just a big round
hut, used on week-days as a school, and the reading
sheets which adorned the walls proclaimed its normal
use. It derives its name from the fact that it is built
on a shoulder of the Bele Mountain.

By this time the congregation has assembled outside, and the ploughshare which serves as a bell was
vigorously beaten by one of the young men. The
people came crowding in until they nearly filled the
hut, and we—Bango, Jack, and I—went outside and
put on our surplices. Out there on the veld, with the
blind preacher and his faithful companion, as we
prayed for the grace and power of the Holy Spirit,
I felt that now at least there was no room for any
critical thoughts. This poor, shabby, sod-built hut
was "none other than the House of God."

We then went inside to sing Mattins. We sang
the whole of Mattins, and we sang more than the whole !
We missionaries have often been charged with the
enormity of forcing the poor, too-compliant Native to
worship God through the complicated forms of the
English Reformation, to the detriment of his natural
faculty for self-expression in prayer. I think it is
true to say that we have never taught Bango to say
or to sing Mattins. Our chief service on week-days,
as well as on Sundays, is the Mass. I have, too,
often encouraged Bango to pray without a form of
words at informal services, and he has always prayed
on such occasions with great readiness. But Bango,
like many other Natives, *loves* Mattins. We may
wonder at it, and we may find it difficult to understand,
but it is true. The truth is, these people, when they
are Christians, must burst forth into praise just as

naturally as the tree bursts forth in springtime into foliage, and they like that praise to be both a corporate act and a "cheerful noise." Mattins seemed to provide them with what they want. Even with the Litany tacked on, and a sermon, they find it inconveniently short!

Speaking of the Litany, I could hardly believe my ears when, at the conclusion of the second hymn, Bango, the *blind* preacher, suddenly started singing the Litany himself, and continued to sing it right through from beginning to end, without book, without a single mistake, and without any hesitation! It was not easy to realise that only a few years ago Bango had been brought as a heathen boy—blind—to St. Lucy's Hospital.

After the next hymn I preached, and I do not think that even Bango can have complained my sermon was short. After the sermon came another hymn, the fourth, and then the blessing. I thought that the service was at an end, but I was mistaken. I was called upon to give out the fifth hymn, and I did so, congratulating myself, I must confess, that there was no place for a sixth. To my great surprise, at the close of the fifth hymn, Bango started singing the *Nunc Dimittis*, and finally, I found myself giving out, by request, the last and sixth hymn! Mattins, with accessories, was now over. After we came out of church there followed the simple *Agape* of the shaking of hands and good fellowship.

As I come to the end of my sketch I ask myself, if I have said everything. Somehow I feel I have left unsaid the one important word. It is the word of One who is not "extreme to mark what is done amiss," who is not on the look-out for faults and failings and discords and imperfections. It is the word of One who delighted to receive honour from the babes and

sucklings in the Faith. This is the word, " Where
two or three are gathered together in My Name there
am I in the midst of them." He who was content to
be born in the stable-cave, does not readily take note
that our church is a very poor one. He who rejoiced
to be called the " Friend of sinners," does not turn
away because our garments are cheap and ugly. He
who did not despise the Hosannas of the crowd, is
not offended because our singing is crude. " The only
measure of all that is ever offered to God is the measure
of the love and self-sacrifice that offers it."

Behind that offering of Morning Prayer at the Bele,
He sees, I venture to think, the stirring of love and
sacrifice. Perhaps it was a " glorified Mattins," but
the only glory sprang out of the love He poured into
the hearts of faithful people. He it is who turned the
water of the very commonplace service into the good
wine of loving worship.

CHAPTER XV

MYRRH

" To see the infinite pity of this place
.   .   .   .
A fool was tempted to deny his God;
He sees, he shrinks.   But if he gaze again,
Lo, beauty springing from the breast of pain."

WE have all seen the picture—the splendid cavalcade, the oriental colouring, the gorgeous dresses, the camels, the serious purpose in the faces of those Eastern princes, and the star, bright, mysterious, alluring. We have pictured to ourselves much that cannot be represented on canvas—the difficulties of the journey, the temptations to be overcome, the strong unswerving purpose. We have thought of the arrival of the cavalcade. They draw near, those Eastern Chiefs, and they stumble not at the poverty and the lowliness of the surroundings. They reverence a mystery of God. They worship the infant King. They present their offerings, gold, frankincense and myrrh.

It is a page out of a far distant past. It is glorious in symbolism. Our artists can paint it upon the walls of our churches. Our poets can sing of it in their verse. But can it be brought near to us ? Even those shepherds aroused from slumber by angelic voices seem less distant to our commonplace matter-of-fact world than those travellers of the East.

ST. LUCY'S HOSPITAL.

ST. CUTHBERT'S CHURCH.

facing p. 10~.

THE BOY'S BOARDING SCHOOL, ST. CUTHBERT'S.

facing p. 103.

So I thought. I was alone in a hut belonging to
St. Lucy's Hospital. It was the Sunday within the
octave of the Epiphany. Every one belonging to the
Hospital had gone to church; the Sister, the nurse,
the Native probationers and the other patients. No,
I am wrong; there was one other patient who, like
myself, was unable to go to church. Obstinately the
thought came back to me again and again. How
beautiful is the story, and yet how remote! It seemed
to belong to another world.

Through the open window I looked out upon the
hills and the Inxu river. My eye travelled up beyond
the forests to the high veld-covered plateau beyond.
I thought of one of our out-station churches which
is on that plateau, but out of sight. It is a building
very much of earth without much to speak of heaven.
At this time Mattins would be in full swing. I could
almost see the preacher, a good homely person with a
comfortable frame and a powerful voice. With great
satisfaction would he lead his flock in singing :

> " Earth has many a noble city ;
>   Bethlehem, thou dost all excel :
> Out of thee the Lord from heaven
>   Came to rule His Israel.

> " Eastern sages at His cradle
>   Make oblations rich and rare ;
> See them give, in deep devotion,
>   Gold and frankincense and myrrh."

Then he would preach. Graphically, far more
graphically than I could, he would describe this journey
of faith, this triumph of endurance, these splendid
offerings. The gold might suggest the golden city of
Johannesburg (i-Goli) with its mines, its wealth, its
wonderful and alluring shops, treasures which might
be brought to the feet of the King. Incense might

suggest a big festival gathering at St. Cuthbert's, the crowded church, the beautiful vestments, the joyous procession. But myrrh ! the myrrh which "foreshows His burial"—what would the myrrh suggest ? I wondered how the preacher would bring this near to the minds of the people.

Suddenly through the open window came the notes of a carol sung in Xosa by a child :

> " They looked up and saw a star
> Shining in the East, beyond them far,
> And to the earth it gave great light,
> And so it continued both day and night.

> " And by the light of that same star
> Three wise men came from country far,
> To seek for a king was their intent,
> And to follow the star wherever it went.

> " Then entered in those wise men three,
> Full reverently upon their knee,
> And offered there in His presence
> Their gold and myrrh and frankincense."

It must be Ciliwe who is singing, the one other patient who had not been able to go to Church. Perhaps she was sitting in the garden under the shade of a tree.

Not so many years ago Ciliwe had been a little heathen child in a heathen home. Somehow or other the Star had been seen in that home. There were no oriental potentates there, no mysterious astronomers. They were just backward, red-ochred, heathen Natives, living in the most complete ignorance of God. Ciliwe had made the venture ; she had followed the Star. She had come as a boarder to the Sisters at the Mission. She had been baptized and confirmed. If any one spoke of Ciliwe it was always as if she at least was a *sure* person. We might be doubtful about this child

or that child, but of Ciliwe there was no doubt. She
was one of those people who even in childhood seem
to be built upon a solid foundation. What she would
ultimately do we did not know. She might be a
teacher, or a weaver, or a nurse, or something else.
But no one doubted what she would be in herself. It
seemed that she had chosen the " better part."

Latterly Ciliwe has often been ailing. Frequently
she had been a patient at the Hospital. It was thought
that her chest was weak, but we hoped that she would
grow strong. And now the verdict has come. We
have been told and she too has been told. Ciliwe is
a leper ! Suddenly she is cut off from home, from
school, from close companionship with friends, from
marriage. She has followed the leading of the Star.
She has found the King. She has brought her offering
—the myrrh of a great sacrifice.

At least this is not remote. The story has been
brought home within our sight. We are allowed to
see a mystery of God—not a pageant but a reality, a
simple child called to follow the Lamb whithersoever
He goeth, even along the most difficult path of depriva-
tion and loneliness and suffering. And as she follows
she sings her song.

CHAPTER XVI

ELLEN MHLAHLELA'S VOCATION

" He lit so many fires in cold rooms. . . . He never could resist stopping anywhere where there was any appearance of loneliness."

DURING the last few years of her life, Ellen's vocation was quite clear. In her case there was no anxious novitiate, no balancing of *pros* and *cons*, no weighing the advice of spiritual guides. God took the matter entirely into His own Hands. Her vocation was not only free from self-choice : it was remarkably exempt from risk of self-consciousness and self-pleasing.

Ellen was brought to St. Lucy's Hospital with severe pneumonia and other complications, and, after a critical period, she made a partial recovery—but very partial. Then the vocation began to be unfolded.

Most people would have said that her life and her life's work were over on the day when she was brought to the Hospital. It is more true to say that they began on that day.

*　　　*　　　*　　　*

It was no light undertaking to plant a Hospital at St. Cuthbert's. I can well remember the day when it was first discussed with the men on the Mission. The Natives are very fond of medicines, and they welcomed joyfully the idea of a Mission-doctor and a

Dispensary, "but we don't understand a hospital."
What is the use of a wife if she can't nurse a man when he
is sick? Does she not promise in church on the day of
her marriage that she will "have" and "hold" him
in sickness as well as in health? And as for the
heathen Natives, we were told that nothing would
induce them to be nursed by the white people.

The younger boarder-boys, when the matter came
on for debate, and they were asked to record their
votes, all with one accord, and with no moment of
hesitation, rejected the counsel of the elders, and begged
to be nursed by their mother in the hour of sickness.
It did not look altogether hopeful, but some brave
people were not easily daunted, and the Hospital was
built.

All was in excellent order. The doctor was there,
the nurses were there, the beds, appliances, surgical
instruments and drugs, were all there. Patients began
to arrive, operations began to be performed, sicknesses
began to be treated. But in spite of every endeavour,
there is no doubt that at first, in the early days of the
Hospital, it was very difficult to overcome that dread
feeling of strangeness in the patients and to make them
feel "at home."

The doctor and the nurses were new to the country,
and, although the former picked up the language with
unusual rapidity, there was at first, in spite of all the
love and the desire to serve, a very big barrier which
time alone could break down, but it was just at the
beginning of things that this particular difficulty was
to be deplored. The Hospital was on trial, and could
ill afford to suffer any disadvantage.

It was then that Ellen Mhlahlela, a Native woman
living on the Mission, was brought to the Hospital.
After an anxious time she began to recover, but before
long it was seen that she was permanently affected,

and that probably she would never make a complete recovery.

For a long time Ellen had been the mainstay of our choir. Her voice was both full and sweet, and it was singularly free from the harshness which is so common amongst the Native girls. It was sad to think that she would no longer be able to take her accustomed place. But she was now to sing the " New Song " in a new way. It happened that Ellen had a remarkably good knowledge of English, and before long she was in continual requisition as interpreter. It might no doubt have been possible to have engaged a regular inter-preter for the Hospital, but this would have been a different thing. Ellen was not merely an interpreter, she was a friend—a friend of the nurses and a friend of the patients. She did not merely translate language —English into Xosa, and Xosa into English; she interpreted *friendship*, and became a very real link between the nurses and the patients.

More than this, little by little she entered into the whole spirit of medical missionary work, and without any official position, without any recognised status at all other than that of patient, she was exercising a real ministry. " We are not strangers here at all, this is home," said a patient to me after two or three days in the Hospital. I noticed that the patient was sitting next to Ellen, and that explained a good deal.

There were many times during those few years when Ellen suffered a good deal, but she was always brave, and generally cheerful. " Can you thank God for your sickness ? " I asked her two days before her death. " Indeed, it is my illness that has taught me most of all," she said; " it is here, in Hospital, that I have learnt the great things." Then, when I had read to her the words which have strengthened so many in every generation, " Let not your heart be troubled, neither let it be afraid," she said, "Now I am strong, I know that I am going Home." On the following day the struggle increased, and made great demands upon the poor heart enfeebled by long illness. But she was still brave, and, although she knew the end was near, she showed great interest when I brought her two letters which came for her by the English mail. It happened that both letters were from friends who had helped to nurse her, and who in their turn had been helped by her.

That day she received her last Communion, and she died while we were all gathered in church to sing the Holy Eucharist on Sunday.

CHAPTER XVII

THE PEACE OF GOD

" At times the mountains speak plainly of One Ancient of Days who was before they began to be ; but too often Nature only echoes back my own moods. . . . The sweet sanctities of home life . . . more often bring me near to the felt presence of God."

IT was a morning of many cares, and they found me ill-prepared to take them smiling. Some of them, it is true, were very small and mundane, but it was the collective weight which oppressed rather than the magnitude of any single care.

" Father, I am sorry to disturb you, but some meat has been stolen out of the store-hut." Reluctantly, feeling very ill-equipped for detective work, I go to the store-hut to compare the meat as it ought to have been with the meat as it is. Then follows a court of inquiry with cross-examination of two suspects. Nothing can be proved, and I am back again in my office. Presently the two suspects come, not to plead guilty, nor even to bring new evidence of innocence, but to take the offensive and to ask why the character of honourable gentlemen should be endangered by false suspicions. They took full advantage of their superior position, and left me humiliated.

Another knock at the door. This time it is Johnson, the excellent " Minister of Agriculture," a Native foreman of farm labourers working on the glebe. I begin by asking Johnson about his chest, which is frequently very troublesome. But Johnson has some more serious news—more serious to his honest mind—than the temporary infirmities of his lungs. One of the Fathers' sheep has died, and Johnson comes to ask what is to be done with the carcase. Remember, we are not in England, where I hope there would be only one answer. We are on the veld where meat is meat, whether the animal has gone to the butcher or whether it has died of disease. I would thankfully have dismissed the question summarily by saying, "Oh, do take it and eat it," hereby bestowing great satisfaction, but I realised the question was a delicate one, and that there were several rival claimants to the carcases of the Fathers' sheep which die. Justice demands investigation.

Another knock. In walks Tinzi, master of the stable—shall we call him "Minister of Transport"? Tinzi is short in stature and not distinguished in appearance, but he has the important charge of a dozen horses and a museum of carts. "Well, Tinzi, what do you want this morning?" "Please, Father, the post-horse is lame with a swollen leg." Not only is veterinary attention required for the patient, but another horse has to be selected to take its place in the post-cart.

At the heels of Tinzi comes blind Bango the preacher. "Please, Father, may I have leave to-day to go and reap my land?" "What do you mean, Bango? Reaping requires sight, how do you propose to reap?" "What I can do, Father, is this. I can sit in one spot where the cobs which are plucked are thrown into a heap, and then I can pull off the sheaves of dry leaves (amakasi)." "Yes, Bango, you may have leave, but did you know that there is a woman in hospital with a broken head?" "No, Father, I

did not know that." " Well, I wish you would go and
talk with her before you go to reap."

So it went on. An ordinary person with a well-
balanced mind and a due sense of humour would have
dealt with all these and many other small matters
with a smiling face and unruffled mind. But, this
morning at any rate, I found things difficult, and I did
not smile. Then it was that succour came, and it
came through Mary Jane.

*　　　*　　　*　　　*

Mary Jane is an old friend of whom I wrote five
years ago, and to-day Mary Jane is very near to the
end of her pilgrimage, and I am going to communicate
her. She is very patient, and, like the very poor all
over the world, makes little complaint of her suffering.
She does suffer ; I can see that in her eyes. I like
to see the welcome of those eyes when I stoop to enter
her little doorway. The hut in which she lives is
perched quite high up on the hill-side, and before I
nqonqoza (" knock " with my voice) I just stand for
one half-minute to take in the beauty of the view.
There is a wonderful sense of restfulness in those
mountains wrapped round by that robe of deep blue
atmosphere which half reveals and half conceals the
outlines. I felt this particularly this morning. It
seemed to me that those mountains are the preaching-
place, the pulpit of Him who once said, " Be not
over-anxious." Through the untroubled peace of those
hills He bids us cast away our care.

I saw the sign. I heard the gracious invitation,
" Come unto Me . . . and I will give you rest." And
yet I could not come. In vain I said, " I will lift
up mine eyes unto the hills ; from whence cometh my
help." Help did not come. I felt as if I were a boat fast
stuck in the mud of some tidal creek. I was waiting
for the tide to lift me up, and the tide did not come.

Just as I was about to knock at the door of the hut, a woman came to beg me to wait a little as they were not quite ready for me. She pointed politely to a little stack of firewood, where I found a seat. It was an exquisite morning. The sun had been up an hour, and already it had beguiled away the white frost which had been gently laid on the grass by a winter's night.

At last Ntombana, the little grandchild, came to tell me that all was ready. As I made my way into the hut by the very narrow and low doorway I caught sight of old Mary lying on her mattress. The dark eyes which looked out from the pinched and drawn face spoke a kindly welcome. I could just hear the one word *Bawo* (my Father) from the half-closed lips. I was carrying with me the Blessed Sacrament, and I knelt down to say some prayers before communicating my old friend. But my movement was regarded as hostile by two hens which were mothering chicks in the hut, and they began to protest with most unnecessary fury. Mary Jane signed Ntombana the grandchild to eject these very turbulent fellow-tenants of the hut. Ntombana seized a long stick to deal with the truants, but this only made matters worse. The mothers took up the battle in earnest on behalf of their much-perturbed children. The noise of the belligerents was almost deafening, and the flapping of wings lifted the white ash from the dead embers of a wood fire and beclouded the atmosphere. To continue kneeling was impossible, so I joined Ntombana, who was evidently quite overmatched. At last, with much triumph, the strangely assorted allies, Ntombana and myself, succeeded in getting the two mothers and, as we thought, all the chicks to the very entrance of the hut, and victory seemed secure. Alas! like the shepherd of the parable, the mother will leave the substantial majority and go after the one that is missing. A frightened chirp from behind a sack of grain reached the ear of one of the valiant mothers, and scorning the combined efforts of the allies she dashed back to the rescue. Then the battle began all over again. Ultimately we prevailed, and the lower half of the door—a Dutch door closing in halves—was shut. With an immense sigh of relief I again knelt down by the side of Mary Jane. I began the confession, followed clause by clause by the old woman. Suddenly a fierce flapping of wings followed by a triumphant cackling announced that one of the mothers was back again. This time Ntombana succeeded alone in dealing with the offender, but it was now necessary to close both halves of the door, effectually shutting out the light. At least darkness and peace were preferable to light and confusion, so instead of reading prayers I " made " them, and then I communicated my friend.

Happily the distractions which had been so trying to me were a matter of small moment to her. Perhaps she had wondered at my desire to eject the fowls. Were they not entitled to a share of the hut ? Perhaps heaven itself would scarcely be homely without the cackle of hens.

Before I left I knelt down and kissed the withered old hand, and I saw a look of great content on my friend's face. It was the " peace of God which passeth all understanding," and it flowed as an ocean tide into my heart. Through Mary Jane succour had come, and my heart was free.